LUCAS ON LIFE 2

'Another firecracker of a book from this master story-teller. Jeff's lucid, often hilarious descriptions of finding God's grace and presence in the midst of the ambiguities of life punch a hole through the masquerade of empty religious formula and help purge us of any self-made image of a distant and unwelcoming God.'

Dave Bilbrough,
International Worship Leader & Songwriter

'*Lucas on Life 2* is funny, moving, deep and like a breath of fresh air. I loved it and read it in one sitting – brilliant!'
Rob Parsons, Director Care for the Family

'Incisive, honest and very funny. Jeff has a way with words that must rank him as one of the best meaningful storytellers of our generation.'

Dave Pope, Director Saltmine

'Jeff Lucas's bite-sized chunks of encouragement come with the authentic flavour of experience. A kernel of truth wrapped in a smile, which leaves a thought behind as an aftertaste. Not a bad recipe!'

Alistair Burt, MP

'Hilarious, warm, penetrating, and human. This book will drive your friends mad – because you will keep reading bits of it out loud to them. But dig deep – there's gold here.'

Ian Coffey – Spring Harvest Leadership Team

Lucas on Life 2

JEFF LUCAS

Authentic
LIFESTYLE

First published 2003 by Authentic Lifestyle.

09 08 07 06 05 04 03   7 6 5 4 3 2 1

Authentic Lifestyle is a division of Authentic Media, 9 Holdom
Avenue, Bletchley, Milton Keynes, Bucks, MK1 1QR, UK.
Distributed in the USA by Gabriel Resources,
P.O. Box 1047, Waynesboro, GA 30830-2047, USA.

British Library Cataloguing in Publication Data
A catalogue record for this book is available from the British
Library.

1-86024-240-5

Cover design by David Lund.
Printed in Great Britain by
Cox and Wyman Ltd., Reading, UK.

DEDICATION

To Kay
my smiling, beautiful, patient and prayerful best
friend,
and beloved wife of 25 years.

CONTENTS

ACKNOWLEDGEMENTS

My thanks to the editors of *Christianity and Renewal* and *Compass* magazines, in which some of this material first appeared.

And to Malcolm Down and the wonderful team at Authentic for their nail-biting patience while waiting for this manuscript.

To Mark Finnie for the chat at Eastbourne, and more.

To Dary and Bonnie Northrup, who deserve joint honorary doctorates for their remarkable gift of encouragement.

To Josh and Sherri Zanders, quiet veterans of faith and grace, who shared the life, and homecoming, of their beloved Tyler with me – and with you.

And finally, my thanks to Alan Johnson, for encouragement, support and diplomacy . . . thank you all.

INTRODUCTION

A FEW WARM WORDS OF GREETING

Before you ask, no, that's not my mugshot on the front cover. I can't tell you how many bright sparks picked up a copy of *Lucas on Life 1* and remarked that the character on the front looked a bit like me. In fact, it seems to me that I am a collector of these kind of affectionately personal jabs. One lady wandered up to me after I had preached and enquired as to whether I had ever suffered a stroke, seeing as, she said, 'when you smile your face only goes up on one side'. I do indeed have a grin that is, shall we say, crooked. I think it was knocked out of true when, at the age of ten, I got a plastic carrier bag caught in the front wheel of my bike, flipped over the handlebars and kissed the pavement at speed.

'No, I haven't had a stroke', I wanted to warmly reply, 'I'm just seriously ugly darling – what's your excuse?' Of course, I said nothing of the sort, but my prospects as an international male model are rather limited. I'd actually like to look like Tom Cruise, or the handsomely elderly Pierce Brosnan – and when I see them in films I wish that some of these smoothly-chiselled chaps could just trip over and get a broken nose like mine (I can smell round corners), but alas, he who stirred the gene pool decreed it not to be.

And I'd *love* a full head of hair, instead of the elderly broom with a growing pink peninsula at the front

13

hairstyle that I'm stuck with. I used to have a flourishing head of hair, with a big bouffant that stuck out at the front. Children and small animals would shelter beneath its shade. But it's all gone now, vaporized by the years and too much bewildered head scratching. The only good thing about my hairstyle is that no one ever accuses me of wearing a wig. Believe me, you wouldn't buy a wig like this!

Alas, life is just not fair. Why is that Steve Chalke so utterly good looking – and such a nice chap who loves God too? It's just appalling: at least I can look at the handsome, multi-millionaire film stars and tell myself that they're not really happy, what with their superficial living and all (though most of us would fancy a go at a superficial life on board a twenty-million-pound luxury yacht) . . . but my friend Steve is handsome, successful *and* he's got God. And I'm supposed to be thrilled about this . . .

And I'd quite like to be a bit sporty, even in one of the less energetic pursuits, like golf. Recently I managed to drive a ball into, not one, but two luxury golf course homes – and they were at right angles to the tee – no mean feat. My hopelessly sliced ball went sailing towards a huge – and correspondingly expensive – plate glass window. Much covering of eyes and falsetto screaming in prayer (if indeed 'Oh my God!' qualifies as intercession) ensued. The ball bounced deafeningly, but harmlessly, on the tiled roof of the first home, and then, so as not to leave next door feeling left out, rebounded with a deafening rat-a-tat-tat on their roof too. I felt led to leave the area quickly. I received no trophies that day, although I did come second place in a church golf tournament recently, and even won a prize. I was feeling quite good until I realized that my three teammates had selected me because they were known as such great golfers, and felt that having me along would provide a perception of a helpful handicap. Oh joy: I am thus designated as excess baggage carted along to even out the odds. I performed my task of messing up their scores admirably, but with me on board, we still came second, which must make them the stuff of Tiger Woods.

Away with these superficial and temporal ambitions. Let's talk about *spiritual* stature. I quite fancy a new description that is currently in vogue: 'Christian Statesman'. Mmmm. Sounds very dignified, and highly noble. But it won't happen. Often when I meet people for the first time they start to laugh out loud immediately they meet me: perhaps it is the nose . . .

I'd like to be Martin Lloyd Jones (but not dead), and be an erudite preacher of unfathomable depth who can whip up an extended 78-part sermon series on the 'Buts' of Matthew, as quickly as Jamie Oliver can rustle up an egg soufflé . . . but again, it was not so destined.

I'd like to be widely quoted, a sage of wisdom. Move over C.S. Lewis and G.K. Chesterton, here comes J.R. Lucas. I got close recently when a friend of mine decided to do a little reading from the first *Lucas on Life* during a service in which we were both participating. (I won't name him, because I promised Rob Parsons that I wouldn't embarrass him.) There's a little moment in volume one where I talk about the danger of losing my *virginal* faith. Rob – lovely Welsh voice thick with drama – read it a little differently, and had me losing my *vaginal* faith. There was a deafening sound around the hall as everyone's buttocks immediately slammed together, followed by the noise of mass choking created by good Christian folk shoving Bibles into their mouths to prevent waves of laughter. There goes my epic literary moment. Sage? Sage and onion more like.

Without, I hope, sounding like Frank Sinatra (*My Way* and all that tosh), I'm just me. A faintly idiotic bloke who

gets himself into more than his fair share of embarrassing
scrapes, clumsy mishaps and scenarios reserved for twits.
I find some of the more 'simple' procedures of life to be
quite difficult – like opening a door, for example. It's supposed to be easy. But I always push when I should pull,
pull when I should push, don't twist the handle when it
should be twisted, and if there's the horror of *double* doors,
then I try to open the one that is bolted shut. Is anyone else
out there as prolifically dysfunctional with doors as me?
Having spent a good ten minutes trying to get into a
homely-looking antique shop recently, I finally gave it an
over zealous shove and landed up flat on my face on the
coconut matting within. The little old lady who owned the
shop peered above her gold half-moon glasses and knit-
ting, and commented dryly, 'Yes, dear, it is a bit difficult,
isn't it?' My friends rolled around laughing, as I had
unwittingly provided the free entertainment, *yet again*.
There's a simple conclusion: I am fairly stupid.

I even have big trouble with those little plastic bags on
rolled dispensers that supermarkets provide us to gather
our vegetables in. Is it only me who finds opening the
pesky things a big problem? They are surely superglued
together by evil people who want to destroy my peace and
patience, or so it seems. Yesterday, the basic and brainless
pursuit of a couple of tomatoes and a cucumber was
turned into a lengthy nightmare of embarrassment. I stood
there, fumbling around, trying to crinkle the top of the
plastic bag open for about ten minutes. It felt like five
years. People walked by and saw my frantic fumbling,
bowing their heads to cover their mocking eyes. One chap
who had 'A' level bag opening wandered up to my side,
ripped a single bag off the plastic roll (when I did it twenty of them landed at my feet and the roll fell on the tomatoes) and then opened it in a millisecond, one-handed – he
was surely a master of dexterity. I flushed tomato red and

mumbled my pathetic excuse, 'These things are a real pain aren't they?' He looked at me like I was the vegetable, like *I* should be in the bag. Yep. I'm a bit sad really.

But I do like to think that I do quite well as a people watcher. I love to mull over the laughter and tears that make up life. And I enjoy telling my little stories, as my friends and family will tell you – having heard them billons of times over, and having been healed many times of insomnia as a result.

So, if you have already read the first volume of this series, thank you for coming back: I commend your fine taste in Christian literature. And if not, you're ahead of yourself. But buy this anyway, and then buy the other one – and then buy 63 for your friends.

One other disclaimer: my view of life is admittedly tiny. It's very much a western worldview; has seen very little pain to shout about; and much of it is spent in aeroplanes, commuting backwards and forwards every three weeks to the USA – hence a fair amount of my episodes being conducted at 36,000 feet. But allow me to share some bits of it with you.

May you laugh a little, cry a little, and think a lot. And may you know that God really does think you're quite marvellous – that's *you*, and the 'you' that you are right now. And if you've never met him before, he requests that I tell you something very important. He would love you to get to know him. A meeting is recommended; I can only write my little snippets about life – *he* is life itself. He wants to sort out the things that come between you and him if you'll let him. He knows everything there is to know about you – and yet he still loves you.

Happy travels.

Jeff Lucas

ATTITUDES

GOD'S ODD PEOPLE

Like a pesky mosquito flying an endless sortie around my head, a nagging thought that just wouldn't be swatted buzzed around my brain last Sunday. I looked around the congregation that I was with, and wondered. Why were so many of these people so downright odd?

This approach is unusual for me. Most of the time, I scan the backs of the heads of my fellow worshippers and feel inferior. They, I reason, are surely far more godly than I. While I struggled to read a single Proverb this morning, they have surely imbibed great chunks of the book of Numbers – and memorized them to boot. While I am fogbound in the Chicago airport of spirituality, and peer hopefully, and occasionally hopelessly through the mire, they have a digital wide screen super-sharp billion-pixel vision of Jesus and an ISDN always-connected/super speed download capacity for prayer.

But this morning, I wondered: what a strange lot my fellow Christians are. That chap over there who wears sandals – and, worse still, socks with them – year round, even through the snowy months. That enthusiastic brother at the front who insists on dancing in the worship even though it is to the unmeaty sound of an acoustic guitar, and even through slow songs like *He is Lord* – is he keen, or just not well? That lady with a hat that is in fact a straw fruit bowl stuck on her head, wearing it as she does in the belief that Jesus wants her to and the sun should be eclipsed anyway – she's very much here, but is she 'all there'?

It's an uncharitable notion, and I feel waves of guilt as I confess it, but why are so many of God's crowd just so weird? It got worse. I wondered: is church just a stained glass holding pen for a whole herd of the weakest links? Are we theologising what is really just a social need for losers to hang together? Would they still come if we sang songs of worship to goldfish?

Before you rush a letter to the Publisher (who, by the way, is a Christian but does not hold his specs together with sticking plaster *à la* Jack Duckworth), let me say that I have repented of my uncharitable musings. I still am nervous when I meet Christians who were blatantly committed to being boring souls before they met Jesus, and in all the years that they have been around him, the most exciting personality in the Universe, they have maintained that commitment to dullness. But I have realized that I was very wrong in my judgement.

First of all, the kingdom of God *is* for losers. Never mind the superficial surface evidences – like so-called fashion or style – of what it means to be a sad type. We are, all of us, invited to join God's party on the basis of our admitting that we didn't make the grade – not that we breasted the tape with pride. Thank God, his banquet is not a garden party for the successful and the smooth. The broken-down, need to get out more / came in last types are offered a seat of honour at the King's table. Far from being an Ascot races enclosure for the loaded, fashionably beautiful top dogs, the kingdom offers a free pass paid for with blood for those who would normally be left shuffling around outside, or invited only in order to use a broom to sweep up the winner's mess.

And then, who can quantify what a loser is anyway? Church is not the arena of the cool types, who strive to

get cooler in Jesus' name. The superficial badges of
appearance and competence that we have to wear to fit
must be left at the door. Those who are called 'nerds' out
in the icy world are welcome, but once inside, around
the Father's warm hearth, the word 'nerd' is banned. All
are invited here, whether you look like me or if you are
mistaken for Richard Gere. In this kingdom of under-
achievers, only the style police are banned, and even
they can come in if they will just put down their trun-
cheons.

The lonely, those who bumble nervously and incoher-
ently at parties – and don't often get invited again
because of it – are at home here. I can fit right in – and
not because I have now decided to wear all-season sandals. It's because of the knowledge that we're all messed
up – all have sinned – and the call to us all is to come into
Dad's house, where the lamp of welcome still burns in
an upper window.

God is the champion who chooses the awkward,
gangly-limbed players for his soccer team, and gives
them equal honour to the Beckhams. He is the swash-
buckling romantic who kisses the 'plain Janes', and
insists on utilizing ordinary people for his purposes and
blessing them in the process. One reason for his heart for
the ordinary is simple – ultimately, we all are.

Ordinary. But much loved.

And, before you go, take another look at the chap with
the socks and sandals combo, and you'll catch a glint of
gold. He's fought a year-long bout with cancer, and lost
his wife a decade ago. He trudged his way through a lot
of heartache and pain, but he's still worshipping from
the top of his head to the soles of his sandaled feet. Looks
like a real winner to me.

THE BRITISH DISEASE

I've said it before, but we Brits are frightfully good at being negative. (Can I say that without being negative?) There are times when I fly into Heathrow and feel as if a great wet blanket of pessimism has been dropped on me from a great height as I walk into the arrivals area. Everyone seems to own a facial expression that implies that they are in need of much bran, because they haven't had a good bowel movement for decades, or so it seems. Perhaps it's our dark, satanic weather: a nation with a summer that doesn't usually last more than forty-five minutes or so has a right to be a bit glum.

A leading politician recently bewailed what she calls 'the great British disease' of negativity. She's right. Our negativity is not only evidenced in our turn of phrase: we're never doing 'well' – rather, we're 'not too bad' (not good, that would be wildly superficial) or we 'can't complain' (we'd love to, and there'll be something just around the corner that will justify a strop, but in the meantime, we wait in anticipation), but also in the bizarre reality that we seem to want people to *not* succeed. We celebrate the underdog and savage the achiever. We are nervous and suspicious of the successful. Is it just jealousy thinly veiled?

And then there's the way that we greet – or *don't* greet each other. We are fairly gifted in the art of totally ignoring strangers, feeling that someone who actually speaks to us without the preface of a formal introduction is, at best, somewhat forward and therefore rather iffy. At worst, this verbose person may well be a roving pervert and therefore worthy of a stoning, or, at least, stony silence. Pity the bored passenger who tries to kick-start a conversation in a railway carriage. He is viewed with the suspicion normally reserved for an escaped felon. And so we ride in lifts, rock backwards and forwards hanging to straps on the tube, and generally go about life without much acknowledging of each other's existence. Of course, I'm not suggesting that life should be going from one little jaunty chat to another with all and sundry, but an occasional moment of kinship wouldn't go amiss.

This is not just a secular problem. I have experimented with saying 'Hello' to strangers at a number of Christian conferences. I occasionally like to catch people's eyes and then offer a warm, 'Good morning'. The response, or lack of it, can be astounding. Time after time, people respond by giving me an 'away from me, you grubby deviant' look, or they just ignore me altogether, which of course is their right, but isn't it a little strange? A couple of times, having been totally stared down and coldly ignored, I wander on, and am tempted to say quite loudly, 'Alright then, *not* good morning . . . '

And negativity can have more significantly damaging effects: it can turn you into a hunter who is always looking for a prize problem. I discover Christians who are constantly on the lookout for something to be upset about in their churches. Life for them is a long, tiresome safari in dogged pursuit of the next irritation. They attend church meetings subconsciously hoping and almost praying that there will be something that will displease them and trigger yet another opportunity for a good gripe. I reckon that they have actually been offended from birth and were probably quite upset with the midwife's welcome. 'Don't you slap me . . . '

Where does this virus of negativity come from? Is it a leftover from a World War II generation that were bombed into believing that there might not be a horizon beyond their horror? They certainly had every reason to lose hope, as they cowered in underground stations during the Blitz, and dared not expect too much. Have we, a younger, unbloodied generation, embraced some of their stoicism, without ever having experienced the horrendous pressures that they faced daily? Are we just boringly negative without cause, we who, half a century later, have never had it so good? Loaded under our mountains of videos, Game Boys, holidays in the sun and a host of other stuff, we're still nervous of being happy?

One antidote for the negative bug is encouragement and affirmation. A friend of mine has, in my opinion, the greatest gift of encouragement I've ever seen. He's the type of chap who would be great in a crisis. If you were unfortunate enough to get your feet run over by a truck, not only would he drive you to the hospital, but he'd also offer to buy your slippers. He can always be relied upon to come up with some jaunty comment to help bring a little sunshine into an otherwise dingy day.

We were playing golf together recently. My golf is totally appalling, and should probably be videoed for a 'look at this useless twit before he took this golf training' kind of product. My swing is not so much a swing, as an involuntary spasm. I teed off and promptly drove the ball right into a lake. I was not happy, and was tempted to mutter an expletive like 'Oh dear!' when my friend jumped in with a smile as big as the bunker that I had narrowly missed on the way to the water feature.

'Great shot, Jeff', he exuded, slapping me on the back.

'Now I know that you are a superficial, cheesy-type person who says absolutely nothing of substance or authenticity', I cried. How could he congratulate me on such a dreadful performance?

I reminded him of the facts. 'Look, I just hit the ball straight into the water!'

'You did indeed . . . but Jeff, you just *hit* the ball . . . '

Sad as I am to admit that just connecting club to ball constitutes a golfing triumph for me, he was right. In that sense, it was a great shot, because it was a *shot* – no matter its ultimate wet resting place. And so, encouraged to keep going, I am currently taking lessons that will help me place a little ball in a small hole from ever increasing distances. Encouragement nudges me to give it all another go.

Let's build churches that are truly counter-cultural – and not just because we dance to unaccompanied acoustic guitars. Let's raise our glasses in gratitude, make affirmation and thankfulness our common currency, and do our best to try to catch someone doing something right. That way, we'll represent Jesus better. After all, he is the one who promises to cut the ribbon of eternity by greeting his faithful ones, not with a could-have-done-better list, but with a simple two-word welcome:

'Well done!'

EVERYBODY NEEDS A KISS

He was a retired headmaster: a ramrod-straight, staunchly moral chap, whose starched shirts seemed to express his creaseless morality. We could always count on him to contribute to a prayer meeting. His prayers were rich tapestries of praise, skilfully woven words of adoration mingled with scripture, spoken in a quaint, Edwardian style, overlaid by his rich Yorkshire accent. Yet there were never speeches of the 'pray and display' kind. Underneath his awesomely white shirts beat a tender heart for the Lord Jesus.

I was just twenty-one, and a fledging pastor. 'Visitation' meant that I was obliged to pop in and see the older folks once in a while. I would listen to their aches and pains litanies, drink endless cups of milky tea, and then peddle on to the next house. I desperately tried to be sympathetic to their rheumatic challenges, but still listened to their problems with the immortal ears of youth. I always felt slightly uncomfortable in the role, trying somehow to be a shepherd to people who'd been on the planet four times longer than I had. My clerical collar rubbed uncomfortably on my neck, like a shiny fairy liquid bottle biting into me and causing me to sweat; sometimes my role as a minister felt like it chafed and rubbed as well.

I used to visit the elderly headmaster and his wife occasionally, and the routine never changed. I would sip my tea and blather on about nothing relevant, and he and his lady would listen, bright eyed and attentive, as if I was dispensing pearls of wisdom like Solomon on a good day. Our time at an end, I would pray for them both, but before I was allowed to leave, he would always ask the same question: 'May we pray for you, Pastor?'

And then he and his wife would come and stand by the green sofa, and place their hands gently upon my head. For twenty minutes, they would thank God for me and ask for blessings of every conceivable variety. Finally, when it came time to say goodbye, he would hug me, and place a kiss on my cheek.

That kiss meant a lot. That man was a scholar of scripture; he could have easily taken my sermons apart, sentence by sentence, leaving them like a shattered Meccano set on the floor. He could have told me about other churches that he'd been part of through the years that were stunningly effective – far more so than our own. And he could have used our time to let me know that the music in our meetings was too loud/long/unfamiliar/unhelpfully accompanied by drums.

But instead, he kissed me.

The elderly headmaster is currently weaving together prayers in heaven. He died years ago, but I still feel the light impression of his tender kiss on my cheek. And on darker days, I touch my face and remember, and I am stronger because of his enduring yet simple legacy.

Everyone needs a kiss.

VIVA LA DIFFERENCE!

French was never my subject at school. My longsuffering French teacher, Mr Ernie Peckett (his real name, believe me), finally booted me out of the class because I got my French salutations wrong. I wanted to attract the attention of the spotty youth who sat at the desk in front of me. Instead of greeting him with a jaunty *'Bonjour Monsieur!'* I cut to the quick and jabbed him in the left buttock with a compass point. The wounded chap, not consoled by the fact that he had pierced flesh twenty years before it became fashionable, roared his protest in English, which signalled my final exit from the class.

So it is that I am now, like many English people, able to say *please* and *thank you* in French, and little more. Oh, I can also ask the time in French – but this is of little use, as I have my own watch. And I can ask for directions to the railway station – and knowing the way to *la gare* would have been helpful on a number of occasions – but I wouldn't be able to understand the reply, unless it involved some linguistically neutral pointing.

So I do what most English people do in France – I speak English with a French accent. *'Ello, ow arr yooo'* I enquire, my tone a hybrid of Maurice Chevalier and Peter Sellers. I usually tack a triumphant *Monsieur* on the end of every sentence, which is cool unless the person with whom I am conversing happens to be female. Thus, my trip to Paris this last week was a series of embarrassing gaffs with more arm waving than a windmill. I did try to ask for a chair in a café – but it turns out that I actually asked to sit on a dog. Most Parisians I met smiled graciously when I apologized for my lack of French, and spoke fine English themselves.

One morning, I observed the antics of a herd of fellow English tourists – and felt ashamed. They were mimicking, in high-pitched parrot fashion, the Frenchman who was trying to sell them a Metro ticket. Obviously graduates from the Alf Garnet School of International Diplomacy, they were totally aghast – appalled even – because this gentleman didn't speak English like themselves, despite the screamingly obvious fact that they were guests in France – *his* country.

Quite simply, they were of the opinion that everyone should look and sound like they looked and sounded. Lurking beneath their crass behaviour was the deception that to be different is to be inferior. Kindly conform, or you are ever so slightly less valuable and significant than we are – for we, after all, are normal – or so the deception goes.

Religion often creates colourless uniformity. Those zealous bloodhounds, the religious leaders of the day, were always hot on the trail of Jesus. His main crime was that he was so *different*. They sniffed the scent of his uniqueness, and bayed like dogs. But, totally refusing to conform to *their* expectations, Jesus marched to a different drumbeat, one tapped out by his Father. At every turn, they tried to smother him with sameness, and desperately sought to buckle him into their religious straightjackets. They failed. Winsome escapologist that he was – and is – he not only resisted their cloning, but called his friends and followers to a life of studied nonconformity. He repeatedly spoke out about the bland pseudo-spirituality of the 'teachers of the law' in the Sermon on the Mount. His call? *'Don't be like them.'*

I am very guilty of religious control-freakery, being more comfortable around folks who worship like I do, who share a common view of how church leadership should be structured, and who use the same general charismatic vocabulary as my own. Perhaps that's normal – birds of a feather and all that – but when my desire for comfort causes me to be dismissive of others who don't fit the mould of my making, then blind arrogance has set in.

Sometimes parenting is about an inappropriate corralling of our children in an attempt to turn out little facsimiles of us. Here I blush: sometimes I have mistaken a desire that my children become more like Jesus with a crusade to actually make them like *me*. No letters needed, thanks, for pointing out the Grand Canyon-like gap between my maker and me.

Incredibly, you and I can be guilty of demanding conformity of God himself. Church can be about a frantic attempt to make God fit our box. We frantically systemize him; try to peg him down like tiny people fussing over Gulliver. We who are made in *his* image desperately try to make him in *ours*.

Let's build churches that are truly colourful and diverse communities, where eccentricity is welcomed rather than feared, and where God's one-offs don't need to sacrifice their uniqueness in order to belong. Regimen is for the cult, not the church.

And by the way, my French vocabulary has grown by 30 per cent . . . here's proof:

Au revoir.

THE PERILS OF STUFF

They say that it's one of the most stressful experiences available. Having just gone through the purgatory that is moving house, I'd say that they, whoever *they* are, are right.

Our loft was like the headquarters of Hoarders Anonymous. I stomped around its humid, dusty half-light, and imagined myself sitting in a circle of forlorn looking people, their heads down, each one of them clutching black plastic bin liners stuffed with possessions. 'Hi, my name is Jeff, and I like to keep stuff.'

'Hi Jeff', they replied in unison, folding their bin bags closer to their chests . . .

The loft held few delights or surprises. We found old lampshades that were never attractive at any point in human history, designed by warped individuals who were surely on a hellish mission to make the world a more ugly place. We unearthed broken toys that were way beyond healing, and ornaments that were cracked and chipped, but had been 'too nice to throw away'. There was a Christmas tree with a two-legged plastic stand; it would have taken a miracle for it to look merry again. An old suitcase with a zipper that had lost its zip. Clothing that would look great on Abba. I turned too quickly in the twilight and got a poke in the eye from an old television aerial suspended from the cobwebbed rafters. Deep joy.

There was brief respite when we uncovered the family photographs, which signalled a torrent of oohs and ahhs. We shed a tear or ten over our long lost babies, all grown up now, and cringed at our awful 1970s hairstyles – and wondered if someone had dared us to have that haircut. Questions abounded. Were we deranged and drug crazed when we visited the hairdressers? And why did I buy that suit with the jacket lapels that looked like the wings of a Boeing? Did the whole world look that ridiculous in 1973? How come nobody noticed? Would we look back someday at 2003 photos and suffer a similar nausea?

And so we engaged in the difficult business of getting rid of things. We sent six trailer loads to the dump. And we were able to dispose of some perfectly good things – that were no longer of any use to us. The local charity shop restocked its shelves because of the clear-out, and our daughter raised a good chunk of change for missions by hauling the rest of the stuff to a car boot sale. But the process of shedding was not without pain.

We found out that stuff, even relatively useless stuff, is sticky. It doesn't want to part company with us without putting up a good fight. While sorting, we repeatedly heard the insane whisper: 'You never know when we might need that.' It was a seductive suggestion, momentarily blinding us to the obvious fact that, at that moment that we might need that item, we are unlikely to spend three hours unpacking crates in the loft in order to find it, even if we could remember where we had put it in the first place. The cold truth was simple – the stuff had to go.

It took even more serious willpower to discard some things, and we didn't always win. Some items placed in the 'get rid' pile launched a silent appeal, and were taken back to our bosom once more. We found out that stuff demands an irrational allegiance, an unreasonable faithfulness, even a mild form of worship.

But as the trailer went to the dump, and the boxes to the charity shop, we felt a strange exhilaration. We had successfully negotiated a clear-out – and the somewhat minimalist house that was left seemed to be a reflection of cleared hearts and minds, just a little less cluttered and encumbered.

And perhaps, in bidding so many things goodbye, we had found that we did not have to hoard, like a squirrel sitting on a mountain of nuts. In a tiny way, the power to possess had been challenged, if only a little. After all, we only really rejected the things that were not of value to us: this was no Mother Teresa triumph over materialism. But we took a faltering step, learning a small lesson, an education that the marketers and advertisers don't want us to learn: things are just things; stuff is only stuff. Or, to put it more eloquently, and indeed biblically, 'A Man's life does not consist in the abundance of his possessions' (Luke 12:15).

THE VILLAGE

I won't name it, in case you live there, and put a contract on my life as a result of reading this. It's enough to say that *the village* is somewhere in Dorset. Its picture post-card High Street, flanked with Victorian street lamps and beautiful Purbeck Stone cottages, makes it the stuff of chocolate box lids. We were there for a month in a rent-ed cottage: a cosy 300-year-old nest where we would celebrate Christmas and I would finish this book. Bliss. Perhaps.

Our first step out was to the pub, a helpful twenty yards from our cottage. Reassuringly old, it looked loaded with character and charm. But there was some-thing of an icebox within. I pushed on the great, ironclad door, my heart tinged with the vague, irrational anxiety that I usually feel whenever I enter somewhere unfamil-iar. But my angst was justified. Suddenly, I felt the trauma of not belonging. The bar area was small, one of a series of very tiny rooms, and locals lined the walls, fill-ing every seat, chattering happily back and forth, the ping-pong of life in a small village. Everyone knew everyone. We, of course, knew no one. We sauntered hopefully in, all smiles and nods of greeting, and imme-diately everything went very quiet: the happy conversa-tional buzz silenced; the chilly quiet deafening. Suddenly the bar area where we stood – blocking their view of each other, and effectively preventing any fur-ther chat until we got out of the way – turned into a stage, with us, the unwelcome fools, stranded upon it. I stammered my order, conscious as I was of my hushed audience, their eyes boring holes in my back. A stammered attempt at a warm comment to the barmaid was rejected with a sniff, so we fled with our drinks to the stark, empty little room next door. Tourists were apparently on the same level in the food chain as rodents. We sipped our drinks and organized an impromptu escape committee.

We are mad idiots. Thus, undeterred, we ventured back to the desolate pub the next night. Frosty, the barmaid, refused to give the barest hint of recognition that she had ever clapped eyes on us before. Our 'Good evening' was greeted with a 'Yes?' Never mind the pleasantries, just get on with your order. One of us, in a rash, suicidal gesture, decided to offer a compliment to her.

'This is a very nice pub!' he chortled.

She looked up slowly from her pouring, eyes narrowed, and volleyed back our warm comment like an unwanted hand grenade. 'Well we're not gonna change it!'

Change it? Who implied that any amendments or revisions were needed? This was a *nice* pub – I said *n-i-c-e*. Hello? Utterly defeated, we retreated again to the draughty little room of the night before.

Okay, let's be charitable. Perhaps these folks get utterly fed up with camera toting, noisy tourists messing up their summers, and see their winter as a needed breather, a holiday from holidaymakers.

So we decided to visit the church for their Midnight Christmas Service. We entered the glorious old building, all dressed up, as it was, in the beautiful candlelit bunting of the season, warm and welcoming. Heads craned around as we accepted our hymnbooks; walking 'exhibit As' now. We needed to sit down, somewhere, anywhere, quickly.

Three seats were close, and vacant. And our bottoms were just about to fill them, when a smartly dressed man seated in the row behind the empty seats leaned forward, waving his hands, a look of horror in his eyes. Then I realized with shame that we were taking seats reserved for the stewards who would collect the offering. I muttered a flustered apology to the flapping seat sentry, and herded the three of us off to some safer wooden chairs at the side of the nave. Flushed with shame, I tried to settle my skipping heart down and just focus on worship. Before long, I felt glad that we had braved the seat debacle. The service itself was rich, and the liturgy heartfelt: these people certainly sang their hearts out. All was going swimmingly, until the sermon. The Minister came quite close to actually recognizing that he was talking to real live human beings, rather than delivering a scripted homily to the ancient rafters. But not close enough. I shifted uncomfortably in my seat, trying to be uncritical, but frustrated by the millions of miles that there seemed to be between priest and people; angry at the fact that this could mean a perception that there were light years between them and God.

On the way out, we shook the priest's hand, and he wished us a rather cold-blooded 'Merry Christmas'. I wanted to pause for just a moment with this man, to engage, to ask a question, but I realized that my handshake was one of those 'swing you past me just keep moving please' mechanisms. We stepped out into the dark, the blinking fairy lights in the church porch, an illusion of cheerier sanctuary than had been our experience. But, come on, break out the charity again. The stewards needed their reserved seats. The seat traffic controller was probably trying to spare us embarrassment as unwitting chair squatters. And the priest? He was probably at the end of a dozen Christmassy services, and was looking forward to a fireside sherry with his wife. But I can't help thinking what people who don't know God – or church protocol – would have made of it all. Would they have determined never to darken the old doors of that church again, and, more tragically, have felt that they could never ever fit in with God either?

But all was not lost. The village grocers-cum-post office turned out to be a haven of delights, and not only because of its fresh crusty rolls and crisp newspapers that looked freshly ironed and starched. The owner was anything but stiff; he greeted us like old friends, and chatted happily about village life. One morning, his shop was loaded with people, fussing around the heaving shelves and tiny aisles. I asked him about a coastal walk and the whole store chimed in, a chorus of help and kindness. Not a hint of raised eyebrows or a 'not-more-stupid-tourists' attitude from them, just laughter, directions and jaunty chat.

I closed the door behind me, a little ding of its attached bell a vague connection to yesteryear. And, needing to buy absolutely nothing at all, I suddenly wanted to go back inside again and rejoin the party.

The grocer who is also a postmaster must be very busy. But I wonder if he could possibly take on running a pub – and a church – as well?

LEADERSHIP

ACCIDENTS HAPPEN

The mobile phone rang, and the news was, for a moment, heart-stopping. It was Richard, our son, his voice the alternating screaming falsetto and occasional bass that is reserved for those whose voices are breaking. The news made me want to scream in unison with him.

'Dad! Please come quickly. Kelly and I have had an accident. A man pulled out of a side road and we've had a head on collision. No one's hurt, but the car looks like a write-off. Please come.'

Kay and I drove very quickly to the accident scene, greatly relieved that there were no injuries, but filled with anxiety. Would our two much-loved children be in shock, or suffer whiplash? And secondarily, but importantly, how bad would the damage to the car be? It wasn't ours, but was on loan from a local garage while our less than trusty chariot was being fixed. We pulled up to the accident scene.

Kelly was tearful from shock, Richard, our very own crusader for truth, justice and the American way, was speaking to the police by telephone, and the other driver was surveying his slightly damaged car, hands on hips. Our loaned car was a mangled mess.

I paused for a second before getting out of the car, attempting in haste to just gather my thoughts and calm my heart. Crossing the busy road, I spent a few moments with Kelly and Richard, and then walked up to the driver, trying very hard not to be angry. Apparently, this chap had been the exclusive cause of this little spat, pulling out as he did. When I finally approached him and spoke, my voice was probably just a little too high, too strained. Note to self: when under pressure, drop an octave, lest you sound like a choirboy.

'So, can you tell me what happened?' I inquired, a strong hint of interrogation in my terse voice.

'Well, your daughter drove into me . . . '

And as the driver spoke that one sentence, *your daughter drove into me*, everything changed. Have you ever seen that film *Alien* where that rather nasty green monster suddenly leaps out of the chest of a hitherto fairly nice chap? My eyes narrowed, my heart beat faster, and I became very conscious of my daughter's tears. I spoke again, anger clearly crusting my voice now; the green monster starting to hurt my ribs and rip my shirt.

'What do you mean she drove into you? She had the right of way, you're the one at fault here . . . ' Actually, 'What do you mean?' came out as '*Whatdayamean?*' and that at higher volume than needed. This man was challenged with his sight, not his hearing.

Whereupon, the kamikaze driver got very animated himself, raised his voice to match and indeed exceed the decibel level of mine, and snorted that he wasn't going to talk to me anymore, seeing as he had already decided that he didn't like me. He gently inferred this. 'I don't like you', he said. And with that, he stomped off to his car, got in and slammed the door, and sat there, resolute, his arms folded, his face an angry mask.

I stood there and pondered. This was not good. It was hardly my finest evangelistic moment. Those seminars on sharing Jesus with strangers don't say anything about road rage. One of the boring things about being a Christian is that you're not supposed to be a disagreeable, irritable thug. One occasionally feels like asking for a few minutes off, but it just won't wash with God. I knew that it was time to put things right, and apologise.

I wandered up to his car, and tapped meekly on the window, feeling somewhat like a mobile Jehovah's Witness as I did. He wound the window down and peered at me.

'Hello! It's me again, me who you don't like, and with good reason. Look, I'm sorry', I spluttered. 'I want to apologise if my tone of voice and attitude upset you. Why don't we start again?' I waited for a response: derision, sneering, rejection? Or warm conciliation? I was to be pleasantly surprised. He looked relieved, smiled broadly, and then launched into his own apology – which contained its own shock.

'I'm very sorry too', he grinned. 'Actually, I'm not normally like this – must be the shock of the accident.'

'I'm a bit embarrassed actually', he continued, and then, with his next sentence, he casually dropped a bomb into my lap. He spoke just five words, and my world came to a halt.

He continued, 'You see, *I'm a Minister of Religion . . . '*

My mind raced. Horrors! This was almost a scene of two vicars having a roadside punch up. What if I had selected an expletive (sad as I am to confess that some seem deliciously appropriate for certain moments of pressure) during our earlier exchange? Thank God, I hadn't hit him, or he me! Imagine the local newspaper. 'Two Dog Collars Beat the Heaven Out of Each Other on Roadside.' 'Ecclesiastical Wrestlemania Breaks Out After Road Incident.' 'More Black Eyes With Your Tea, Vicar?' 'Men of God Behaving Badly', and the like.

I was tempted to confess that I was, in fact, a passing plumber on my way to a heavily bunged up sink. Could I perhaps help him with some blocked pipes? No, it wasn't right. Time to confess all. I took a deep breath, and spilt the beans: 'Actually, I'm a Minister too . . . '

'Really? What's your name?'

Yikes. This accident scene was turning into a house-group meeting. I was glad I'd left my guitar at home. Any minute now we'd been joining hands and singing *Kum By Ya* at the roadside, and sharing our burdens. I told him my name, and his eyes widened in unfortunate recognition.

'Jeff Lucas? I know you! I heard you preach at Spring Harvest last year. In fact I bought the video, and was only watching it a couple of weeks ago . . . *so very* nice to meet you Jeff!'

And so, our little moment of conflict (more road *irritation* than rage) was over. In fact, we did have a very nice time chatting, and we were able to drive him across town to pick up his family. And later that night my new-found friend (a Church of England Rector, who surely 'wrecked' our car, boom boom!) very kindly called us to say that he had told his insurance company that the whole thing was entirely his fault and that a claim would be no problem.

I breathed a prayer of thanks that I hadn't acted in a more un-Christian manner than I had . . . but then I started thinking, which is dangerous.

I had been embarrassed at the thought of being a man of God behaving badly and then being caught 'in the act' as a reasonably well-known Christian . . . but does that mean that I could behave in that manner with someone who *didn't* know me? Fortunately, we had both apologized to each other before we got into the clergy reunion part, but I still think that Christian leaders can suffer a particularly strong temptation to be brusque with those that they don't have to be kind to. The rest of their lives are spent in an existence governed by the behavioural expectations of their congregations. They are required by nature of their vocation to smile, listen, be courteous, look interested, be polite, and generally be good at all times.

The chap who won the *Halitosis King of 1983* award needs to be listened to, even at appallingly close range. And Mrs Whatsername who is threatening to execute someone if we sing that nasty new song again on Sunday morning, and whom, you suspect, got chucked out of the Gestapo for being too rough, must be heard: nod, 'Yes dear', 'No dear', 'I understand' . . .

And then we bump into strangers who make no such demands on our limited reservoir of niceness – and then suddenly our theology in a second becomes a theory, and one very different from our actual practice. We can end up with two sets of attitudes: one for Sunday morning, and another for the rest of the week.

How quickly we can lose our integrity, and the authenticity of our faith justifiably comes under question, when we live this Jekyll and Hyde duality. The truth is that that which we say we believe, we live by – all the rest is religious froth. Two timing behaviour is a con. Stern words were spoken by Jesus to the Pharisees, who mastered the art of 'pray and display', but were full of death and corruption within. The obvious truth is that my behaviour should not be monitored by a fear of being caught – but by a desire to treat everyone that I meet as if they were Jesus himself. And that's not just about unwitting strangers: our closest family members are entitled to the same level of courtesy and respect that we afford to Derek the awkward deacon, whom we are silently praying will be abducted by the Taliban. Christian leaders are not called to be quick-change artists or platform chameleons.

So next time that driver tails you closely, impatiently honks his horn and then cuts you up, breathe a prayer for urgent grace, and avoid that temptation to unkind gesticulation – and not just because of *that fish* that sits on your back bumper . . .

CLONES AND BOXERS

The worship time had begun well enough, but now even the most seasoned Duracell-fuelled charismatics were flagging. Arms that had been raised in adoration were slumped now in weariness. The dancers who, thirty minutes earlier were fluid, yet graceful with energy – and dangerous with flags – were still and quiet now.

But the large, overweight worship leader, his belt fighting a losing battle to support his overhanging stomach, was not satisfied that we had done our bit. Heaven was apparently not satisfied yet with our offerings of praise. More specifically, he had no patience for slackers. Jesus was worth praising, 'WASN'T HE?' he roared breathlessly down the microphone. If we didn't raise our voices, the stones would cry out, 'WOULDN'T THEY?' 'EH?'

Like a bunch of schoolboys caught puffing illicit ciggies behind the bike sheds, we nodded our tired surrender. Even the band was a bit fed up with it all. The keyboard player stabbed the first note of the song with a little attitude. I wondered if he was fantasizing about poking the worship leader in the eye.

I go to lots of these kinds of meetings, and enjoy most of them. But every now and again, I feel unutterably weary of it all – and I wonder if perhaps the Lord gets numbed too by our exhausting routines when we actually end up worshipping worship. Let's face it, omnipresence has its drawbacks: I've often wondered if Jesus had ever regretted

promising that when two or three gather together in his
name, *he would be there*.

Now Bubba, the worship leader, had decided that we
all needed to forget about ourselves, our problems, our
lives, and the person next to us (thus negating the reason
for us coming together in the first place – I could have
stayed at home and more easily forgotten about the person who was not next to me) and that we should *raise our
hands together to the Lord . . . right NOW!!*

I looked around the congregation; a silent sigh seemed
to settle in the air. Hands went up in resignation. And
then, marvellously, gloriously, it happened.

The worship leader, his own arms akimbo, had
breathed out one time too many, and his valiant and long
suffering belt buckle exploded with a loud ping that
caused a number of older worshippers to jump. In a second, his trousers slipped down, all the way to his ankles,
revealing a voluminous pair of boxer shorts that were
apparently manufactured by Mr Walt Disney. Mickey
and Minnie, their cartoon arms also raised, perhaps in
worship, were running all over his underwear.
Immediately the poor man reached down in a desperate
attempt to retrieve both his errant clothing and his modesty. The members of the congregation, now an unwitting audience in a striptease, attempted, unsuccessfully,
to be warmly compassionate. Many blinked their eyes
closed, desperately trying to focus on the streets of gold
above. They were so desperate to contain their mirth, but
their eyes were pious slits, and their shoulders shook
quite uncontrollably with mirth.

It was a wonderfully liberating moment, which
became even more bizarre just seconds later. As he fum-
bled with his now retrieved trousers, the worship leader
leaned into the microphone and whispered with an
X Files voice, 'It's amazing what the devil will do to you

when you're trying to lead worship . . . ' Nervous brothers all around the room immediately felt led to check their own belts in order to outwit the enemy in his deceitful scheming.

But the spell of control was gloriously broken. The command that everyone obey, conform, and get in line was shattered by a moment of real life. No longer did we have to be harangued, intimidated, or harassed into yet more uniform singing. The spell, if you will, was broken along with the belt buckle.

Leaders must never lose sight of the fact that God's people are just that – *God's people*. They are not just sheep to be herded, fodder for our vision, or fools to be patronized. They are unique poems written by God. We may exhort, encourage and invite, but those people are just not ours to harass, harangue, and manipulate – they are his. Let's always remember that, when we shepherds are tempted to become ranchers – hollering, herding cowboys – rather than those willing to lay down their lives for the flock. The eastern shepherd goes before the sheep, leading them, not behind them, driving them.

And of course, we should also remember and be diligent in these days of spiritual attack . . .

. . . to double-check our belts.

THE FRIEND NO ONE WANTS

The service had gone well, and I felt that welcome feeling of grateful weariness; the warm glow that comes when you sense as a leader that perhaps you've helped people to walk into another day with a few more handfuls of hope. I strolled to the back of the church building to my book table, ready to pack things away. It was then that I saw it. The note was folded exactly in half, and stood crisp and upright on the book table, militarily demanding attention. My name was scrawled in an angry address across the front of it. Something told me that this was not an epistle of warm appreciation. I was right. A familiar dread turned my stomach to lead as I reluctantly unfolded the note, its creases razor sharp.

The words within were sharper still. I had obviously angered somebody in the congregation, who were certainly not used to the approach that I take to preaching. I love humour, but not all Christians share my desire to smile, and neither do they have to. It's just a shame that some of them become the joyless police, eager to arrest anyone who might possibly be having just a tiny bit more fun than they are, which isn't hard. I am personally committed to the idea that fun is not something that should be (a) reserved for after death for Christians and (b) kept a million miles from biblical preaching. The writers of the note vehem-ently disagreed. Their scribble was like a lurid scar on paper; it screamed their indignant protest. Would you, my dear and inquisitive reader, like to read the note? Okay.

Sir,
We would see Jesus, not your comedy act and nonsensical gibberish. You can't win souls to Jesus with all that rubbish. You are not a preacher – you are a comedian. You have missed your calling.

The terminal diagnosis concerning me was unsigned. This person – or persons – who felt constrained to announce my utter worthlessness had not chosen to reveal their identity.

I folded the note back in half, my heart heavy within my chest. I do know what I'm called to do, and I've been around long enough to know that not everyone is going to like it. The privilege of leadership carries with it the unwelcome moments when we will feel the bitter sting of criticism. But the wildly scrawled note had the effect of a missile on my own sense of hope, blowing my joy to smithereens. I stood there, and wondered about what kind of person could be so hateful in Jesus' name, and suddenly I wanted to not be a Christian leader anymore. In fact, for a second or two I even wished I wasn't a Christian, seeing as these so-called 'friends of God' were such accomplished verbal assassins. Fortunately, my hankering for atheism only lasted a few seconds, before logic rebooted in my brain.

It's never enjoyable to be criticised, particularly when it comes wrapped in the cowardly garb of an anonymous letter; an envelope stuffed with verbal barbed wire. These days, if a letter comes unsigned, I won't give it undeserved dignity by reading it. If the person who wrote it does not have the moral backbone to sign it, then why should I trouble myself reading the fruit of their spineless lack of conviction?

But hold on. Are there times when we leaders are criticized, and too quickly rush to conclude that our critics are just fools? Write off the critic too quickly, and you could be ignoring an unwelcome gift of God to you.

Visionary leaders often find it very difficult to receive even the most constructive criticism. Blinded by our passion to follow what we perceive is a God-given mandate, we brush off words of caution and correction as being born of a lack of faith – or worse, we gleefully suggest that our critics are speaking as unwitting agents of Satan. Surely, we conclude, if we, (like the Blues Brothers) are on a mission from God, then any voice that challenges that mission must find its source from the pit below? This is particularly possible when a church is following a prophetic word that has been given. With simplistic naivety, the leaders determine that God has spoken and so any contrary voice must come from the Satan who loves to distract, conveniently forgetting that the prophetic must be weighed, and that honest, rugged, healthy debate is an essential part of that process.

We then move to the place where anyone who speaks with a dissenting voice *themselves* becomes the enemy, even though they may actually be expressing the true faithfulness and commitment that only comes from the best of friends.

The problem is further compounded if the criticism comes in the high-pitched messiness of an unhelpful attitude. The critic is angry, upset, maybe even spiteful, and so we conclude from the way that the message is delivered that therefore the *message itself* must be wrong, which is like ignoring a letter because the envelope is torn. And so we stumble on, convinced of our own rightness, now infallible evangelical leaders who can't even be corrected by the ultimate authority of scripture. Deception has begun its winsome, seductive dance with us.

We get deeper into the fog when we endeavour to use the issue of local church unity as a weapon to silence dissent. We brand anyone who asks a question as awkward or, worse still, an agent of division. I am staggered by the way that Christian leaders sometimes describe those who have left the churches that they lead. 'God is just purifying the body', they affirm with smug smile, branding the departing people as dross. The worst example of this in my memory was a leader who wrote off some people that had left the church with the words, 'Well, of course, every healthy body needs a bowel movement once in a while' – an arrogant, devastating belittling of people as being little more than effluent. Outrageous.

Let's face it, none of us enjoy criticism, and there are many times when it is unjust, hurtful and a slap in the face for the already weary. Some leaders react as they do to criticism because they are just so punch-drunk; so shattered from the years of so-called friendly fire that they just can't take anymore. But, just as pain is unwelcome, it is actually the gift of God to us if we have placed our hand on a hot stove – and remember that the absence of pain is the blight of the leper – so criticism may be the signaller that we hate to see, but may just save our lives.

I still encourage you to ignore unsigned letters, as long as you have not created a culture in your church where people are too scared to identify themselves with even the most constructive criticism. But, whoever you are, leader or not, be careful about labelling your next critic a fool too quickly. He or she could turn out to be the most faithful friend you have.

FAITH

THE DIVING INSTRUCTOR

Right from the start, I knew that my decision to take scuba diving lessons was a huge mistake. This dawned on me as I poured myself into a rubber wetsuit that had apparently been created for a six-stone supermodel, donned fluorescent yellow fins that were bright enough to be seen from Jupiter, and attempted so dressed to amble nonchalantly to the swimming pool for the introductory session. One is supposed to look relatively relaxed and cool when one is walking by the side of a pool. Ever tried strolling casually while dressed like a fat, beached sea lion with custard coloured feet? I was grateful that no one threw me a fish, but embarrassed that my fins slapped the concrete pool surround with each step, forcing me to lift each foot high before placing it down, the fat seal meets the ministry of silly walks. Very uncool indeed.

The diving instructor was waiting. He was a bronzed gladiator with jet-black designer fins and muscles in places where I don't have places. His flyaway blonde hair was bleached the colour of summer straw by the sun; he looked like a Nordic god. In stark contrast, the top of my flaking head was broiled the colour of a dead lobster by the same sun. As for Nordic, I'd never even been to Norway, and felt like Quasimodo meeting Tom Cruise.

It was time to manoeuvre the heavy oxygen tank onto my back. I fought and struggled for five minutes to get the wretched thing on. The instructor threw his tank up in the air, which landed perfectly on his freckled shoulders. Great.

We completed the try breathing underwater in the swimming pool thing, and so *Thor* decided we were ready for the ocean. Nervously, I climbed into the back of the van that took us to the beach. Then they told me that oxygen would not be needed for the drive. I got out of the van and wrestled my way out of the wretched tank. But I left my flippers on for the journey.

Okay, I admit it. The ocean diving was exhilarating, a jump into another world. Great shoals of fish, sprinkled with rainbow colours, weaved and darted around me in perfectly synchronized dance. A huge crouching octopus held a shadowy court in a cave 120 feet down. During a night dive, we sat on the bottom and shone our underwater torches up, which exposed swirling plankton, a drive through fast food joint for manta rays. Great spaceship like mantas lined up to glide over us and feed in the light, dive bombing us in slow motion, and rubbing their bellies on our heads as they did. With my short, spiky haircut, I was a big hit with the mantas; I'm no male model on land, but in the world of the rays, I'm a pin-up.

Richard, our son, became more and more confident in the presence of the instructor. During the night dive, our thirteen-year-old had got into some trouble. First, a moray eel wrapped itself around his leg, and then one of the mantas got its wing caught up in his scuba gear. Suddenly, he was being swept off into the dark deep at high speed. The instructor, lighting-quick reactions ever sharp, saw the emergency, reached out and disentangled our son in an instant. Richard thought the instructor was great: after all, in a sense, he had saved him.

But then, after a couple of days of diving, the instructor told us something that I believed to be mildly heretical. He said that it was a great privilege for a diver to swim with sharks. There were plenty of Tiger sharks in the area (they happen to be highly dangerous killing machines). Would we like to have a swim with them?

I pondered this offer for at least half a second, and said 'no' in five different languages and accompanied this with much shaking of the head. It was a ridiculous idea. A privilege to swim with predators? Pah! I even looked up 'sharks' in my mental concordance and couldn't find a single biblical verse to support this unscriptural notion. But my teenaged son believed the instructor. Sitting on the boat, he scanned the surface of the waves for sharks, waiting hopefully.

At last, a menacing fin was circling the boat, prompting me to hum the theme music from *Jaws*. 'Look, Richard, there's a . . . '

Splash.

Richard was already gone, over the side, in the water – where the fin was. The instructor went after him. They were gone for about five years – or so it seemed.

I shouted, prayed, begged, and wished that I'd taken up gliding or ferreting. A few minutes later, Richard and the instructor emerged dripping and triumphant. I performed the welcome sequence from the parable of the prodigal son, and enquired as to whether Richard needed psychiatric assistance.

'Dad, don't be daft . . . look, the instructor said it would be okay. And he was with me. I'm fine.'

His philosophy was simple. The man said so. The man is with me. Therefore, I will swim with sharks.

And it seems that Jesus offered us a similar logic when he responded to dozens of questions with just one answer: 'I am with you'.

Sounds clichéd, a throwaway line? Not a bit. This is not bravado or hollow rhetoric, but the assurance of someone who has wrestled death into submission, has stared straight into the sulphuric eyes of Satan, and has declared that he is the one who stands astride death and hell itself.

He is with us, and that knowledge takes us beyond Christian moralism or evangelical activism. It calls us back to a bravery that is not just based in believing the right things, but is centred around the fact that he has committed himself to journey with us. There will never be another moment of aloneness for us who have invited him to be the master and instructor of our lives.

Ponder it and wonder, and look with new eyes at the circling sharks. The man is with you.

PEMBERTON STATION

I was frustrated and angry, and I slammed the front door hard behind me, a noisy *amen* to what I felt had been an exasperating evening. My 'cell' meeting (sounds like I'm an offender) was the reason for the angst: we had spent an hour or so chatting about the supernatural. Two of our number had just come back from overseas travel, where they had apparently witnessed some rather impressive miracles of healing. We had chatted about the need for us to see more genuine Holy Spirit activity where *we* live. I should have been inspired – but was irritated instead. I'm sure that it's rather wonderful for the Chinese church to be raising the dead – particularly if you're Chinese and you happened to be around to see the corpse involved suddenly perk up – but it's not such fun at a distance.

Frankly, being treated to a diet of distant stories about God working overtime elsewhere – or in the past – is a bit like being starving and homeless, and peering longingly through the bushes at a royal garden party. You might start off merely salivating, but after a while, you get a bit outraged at your own lack of cucumber sandwiches. Hence my door-slamming routine. How come, I raged, God couldn't show up a bit more around here? Yes, I know all the but-we-live-in-a-culture-of-unbelief apologetics routines, but why couldn't God help us clear the aforementioned cultural fog with a few faith-building activities that might get our eyes popping and our

63

hearts quickened? As I slammed the front door, I think I closed a door in my own heart as well. I decided that talk of miracles was tiring, and felt the need to bolt and double lock myself off from prophecies that aren't terribly prophetic. I had been in enough charismatic meetings where 'words of knowledge' were given that were less than exciting, and where apparently meaningless revelations were greeted with way too much enthusiasm.

Perhaps you know the kind of thing I mean. In the midst of a mildly orgasmic time of hyper worship, a wide-eyed prophetic type stands to his feet, breathless and slightly ecstatic. Apparently, he has news. 'I sense a breakthrough in the third heaven as we drill through the core of accumulated crustiness with our intercessory Black and Deckers. Yes, there is a well that has been bunged up since Charles I (for it was closed off spiritually upon the death of one of his spaniels; the poor thing expired when the King was passing through this town) – and now it is springing to life again, hallelujah!' What really freaks me out is that everyone who hears this twaddle then feels the need to pretend that they fully understand and resonate with what is being said – although I reckon that, privately, they haven't the slightest clue. I want to stand up and scream: 'What in blue blazes was all that about then?' But hyper-mysticism carries its own force field. When you say that you don't understand what the 'prophet' is rattling on about, people look at you with pity, because you're not one of the spiritual, initiated elite. 'Never mind, dear, you just need to go deeper. One day you'll see what we see . . . '

Do I sound angry? That's because I am. Not only do I get exhausted and demoralized conversing with 'prophets' who are more 'International Men of Mystery' than Austin Powers, but I feel real concern for young

Christians who feel utterly disenfranchised by this Gnostic drivel. And exactly that happened during a 'spiritual' weekend held in a church that I know recently. Brand new Christians came out of meetings feeling like they must surely not be saved, as they couldn't begin to relate to the intergalactic mush that was being dumped on them in Jesus' name.

And I've been on the 'brink of breakthrough' as a result of those 'revival is just around the corner' prophecies for so long that I feel like a mountain climber. Even as I write now, I feel again the quiet sense of rage that caused me to slam the door so hard back then: I was officially retiring from being a charismatic. That was very much that. I stomped off to bed and didn't pray any goodnight prayers. I was in a sulk.

The next morning I awoke with the rasping throat and foggy head of a heavy cold. Wondering if perhaps I might have been smitten by this plague as a judgement for my stroppiness, I decided – having turned my back on healing for good – to request it just one more time.

I tried the various prayer-for-healing approaches that were then in style, beginning firstly with the soft and gentle Californian whisper of the healing prayer, *Vineyard* approach. This is the kind of healing prayer that I particularly like, because it involves no shouting or massaging of anyone's body parts, just a reverentially casual easy does it request that God might do something. I cooed and whispered and prayed that I'd get better, and nothing happened at all.

I decided to switch to the more Teutonic aggression of a Rienhard Bonke Pentecostal prayer. Bonke is a delightful German evangelist, and his prayer style operates on the belief that, while God isn't deaf, he isn't nervous either. Secondary injuries occasionally occur during this kind of praying. You may be requesting relief from earache, but could find yourself with a nasty case of whiplash resulting from the undeniably sincere, but marginally over physical prayer-wrestling that might ensue. I've experienced a few of these fervent punch-ups, during which I've had my ears boxed, my stomach jabbed, and even had a brand new jacket covered in fat because the over enthusiastic ministry team soaked it in truly authentic olive oil from the Holy Land. They did at least realize their error and paid the dry cleaning bill.

Anyway, I placed both hands on my head and roared a rebuke at the cold germs that I felt would surely scare the hell out of the Devil. For two or three minutes I bound and loosed, rebuked, cast out and generally nuked everything I could think of. So Bonke was I, I even found myself praying in a slight Germanic accent. Remember the fat sentry in *Hogan's Heroes* who used to run around yelling 'Raus, Raus'? That was me, commanding the cold to 'Raus, raus!' in Jesus' name. But it didn't want to raus. I said the Amen with a congested sniffle. That night I went to bed armed with a Vicks Inhaler for each nostril, two boxes of Kleenex and a drip feed of Night Nurse. Suffice it to say that faith was not at its highest level. The door, as it were, was slammed, locked, bolted, and I was thinking of nailing it up permanently.

But while most of the time God waits to be wanted, there are occasions when he will come as a loving burglar, scaling our pathetic defensive walls and flicking off our security systems, overriding them with what at first seems to be unwelcome love. The Fatherly intruder came while I slept; perhaps the only time my mind and mouth are still enough to allow him a word in edgeways. I dreamed the same, strange dream over and over – and even as I share it with you, my perplexed reader, I feel like I am broadcasting from the charismatic twilight zone. Bear with me if you can.

In the dream, I was standing on a railway station – Pemberton Station. A railway official stood on the platform and chatted with me while I waited for a train that never actually came. His chat filled me in on all kinds of information about this place called Pemberton. When I awoke, the dream had not evaporated like the morning dew (as most of my dreams do). It was crystal clear, vivid and sharp in my memory. And as I lay there in the warm coma that is called waking up, it occurred to me that I would bump into someone called 'Pemberton' that very day, and that I would tell them what the railway porter had told me, and that it would speak to them of hope, and of better days ahead. This was unusual, strange, and would take a major bit of acrobatic organization from God to make such a thing happen – especially as I had never met anyone called *Pemberton* before.

I was due to speak at 'Equipped to Lead', a day of leadership training that would be attended by around sixty people – not exactly a cast of thousands from which to pick a Pemberton. I drove excitedly to the hall where we were due to gather, rushed in and grabbed the list of pre-registered delegates. My feather-light heart turned to lead as I scanned the list and my eyes hurried down in search of *P* for Pemberton. There were none present. It was like a bad taste in my mouth, yet another disappointment to compound my feeling that locked doors were good doors. If faith were a vital sign, I would have been pronounced dead at that moment.

Just before the first session was due to begin, a breathless couple walked quickly up to the registration table, and announced that they wanted to join the course, and that they hadn't had a chance to pre-register. Would it be okay? I smiled my agreement, asked for their names, and almost fell over. They were Mr and Mrs Pemberton.

I think I said something giftedly stupid like 'Nice to meet you, I was on your station all last night', but then asked if I could talk to them in the break. I couldn't believe it – suddenly belief was believable again.

I got to tell them my British Rail dream, which they said made good sense, but I asked them to think on it, share it with whoever they wanted to (I do believe in personal prophecy – but not *private* prophecy). We laughed and cried some together and they telephoned me a few weeks later to say, yes, they had thought, prayed and shared the word I gave them with trusted friends, and did feel that God had clearly spoken.

Lest this chapter end with everybody living happily ever after, with John Wayne riding over the sunset-kissed hill on a grinning horse, let me give a little postscript for your prayers, if you will. A prophetic word is not a sick note from God that excuses and exempts you from trial. The Pembertons have faced health challenges in recent months – please pray for them, if you will. But I cannot deny the fact that, when I was worn out and faithless, ready to jump the charismatic ship for good and wave goodbye to the gifts of the Holy Spirit, that God picked my lock, and my brain, and beautifully broke through my little defence system.

I still crave a bit more quality control – and some honest talk – around the prophetic. But my pendulum swing of unkind dismissiveness and outright hostility to God was wrong. Burglars from heaven are welcome. Better still, don't slam that door.

UNREALITY

The service was over, and I was enjoying the warm afterglow chatter over a cup of tea. The man approached me, a broad smile on his face, but a slightly nervous look clouding his eyes. 'I need to ask you a question, if I may', he ventured. I nodded my willingness to be so quizzed. In these moments of after service encounters, you never quite know what's going to be on the agenda. He looked around furtively, as if he was about to confess that he had taken part in the Great Train Robbery or was an undercover mass murderer. I braced myself. I've heard more than my fair share of lurid confessions. Throwing all caution to the winds, he launched into his question.

'Is it alright if I say that I have a headache?'

My brow wrinkled in confusion. This was not the anticipated whisper of shame and degradation. He just wanted to know if a dull pain in the brain was admissible. My reply was careful.

'Well, let's start at the beginning. Do you *have* a headache?'

He looked down as if I had enquired as to whether he was a carrier of a sexually transmitted disease.

'Yes, I do.'

'Well, if that's the case, it's okay for you to say that you have a headache.'

By now, I had things figured out. I guessed that this man was from one of those churches where Christians are not supposed to get sick, ever. Bouncing from one

victorious mountaintop to another, these folks espouse
the notion that Christians should never ever be without
health or wealth. Of course, there is a rather pressing
problem with all of this, and that is that Christians *do* get
sick (in fact, a few of us have been known to die, rather
like the rest of the human race). And our bank balances
aren't always in the bold black, even if we tithe, bless the
missionaries *and* send a few quid to that loud man on the
television who says that supporting his ministry is a
sure-fire pathway to raking in the cash for ourselves. But
the idea is that we are not supposed to admit that we are
walking through the mire of these problems: to do so is
an admission of the failure, and so we are supposed to
make a *positive confession*, and speak into being that
which is not. Thus, any time we say that we are sick, we
are speaking into reality our own sickness, rather than
speaking words of faith. Headaches are thus forbidden.

Bad theology is a harsh taskmaster; people have been
known to die as a result of embracing this space cadet
approach to life. But there is a less obvious, yet sinister
side to this idea of positive confession. When you live in
a regime of required victory, unreality will not just be
contained in the way that you give a health report. Like
a sparking car battery, unreality will jump across the ter-
minals of our lives into all kinds of other areas where we
are in need, yet feeling the need to deny our difficulty.
Our morality can come into this cloud of pretence.
Feeling desperately unworthy about ourselves, and
knowing that we have all kinds of secret sins rattling
around as the proverbial skeletons in the cupboard, we
'confess' that all *is* well, as if our saying so means that all
is well. In effect, we lie, and all in the cause of keeping up
the façade of faith. Sins are thus buried deep, undiscov-
ered until a day of disaster (or deliverance?) when
finally we get caught and light cascades into the dark

dungeons of our own construction. But where God's reign – the kingdom – is, there will be truth, even if the truth is uncomfortable and unpalatable.

John the Baptist, that odd chap with strange fashion choices and stranger dietary habits, baptized the crowds in the wilderness, building a motorway for Messiah to travel on, and as he did, the people yelled out their sins just before they went underwater. Why? Well, the King was coming – it was time to get real. And fellowship is about reality and truth. Often, a 'time of fellowship' is reduced to a quick handshake for thirty seconds during our 'services', where hymn singing is top priority, but actually, being together and sharing the good and bad bits of our lives is further down the food chain of priority. Walking in the light, to borrow John the Apostle's terminology, is the pre-requisite of fellowship. That doesn't mean that every time someone asks us how we are we should produce our medical records, x-ray charts and actually tell them, but it does mean that we ensure that there are those who truly know us, and who have permission to help us to know ourselves, as we allow them to rebuke, comfort, challenge and question us. Jesus sobbed in the faces of his friends and followers and said that he was totally overwhelmed in the garden of Gethsemane. And even the somewhat stoic Paul informed the contentious Corinthians that he had perhaps been tempted to suicide, 'we despaired even of life. Indeed, in our hearts we felt the sentence of death' (2 Cor. 1:8–9). Hardly the stuff of grinning positive confession.

The irony is that reality seems to be connected to healing. James exhorts those with headaches, and more, to call for the elders of the church and request prayer, but slap-bang in the middle of all that supernatural stuff, he tells us to confess our sins to each other as well. Perhaps we would see more miracles if we could just be a little more authentic.

So, yes, it's all right to have a headache, be fearful, angry, have tumours, and indeed experience a whole bunch of pains from which Christians are certainly not exempt. Perhaps, if we could just get a little more real with each other, we might find some of these things actually being shifted by heartfelt, faith-tinged and honest prayer.

ON THIN ICE

It was a beautiful, crisp, autumnal day, the bright sunshine disguising the deadly reality of black ice lurking stealthily on the road surface. We were driving up a mountain pass in Oregon, a million Christmas trees creating a lush, green carpet below us. As we snaked up the pass, I observed that one should avoid the edge of the road, for there was a sheer drop of hundreds of feet; no crash barriers were to be found. The philosophy behind this road layout was simple – drive carefully or die.

A friend was at the wheel. I was in the back of the car, wrestling with our young children who wanted an 'are we nearly there yet' update every thirty seconds. Suddenly, as we steered round a rather tight bend, we hit a patch of frozen ice (note for non-physics graduates: most ice is frozen). The car went into a spin, and I casually observed that we were moving across the road towards the gaping snow-white jaws of oblivion. This was not good, could not be the will of God for us, and even if it was part of the plan, I didn't like it. I decided to express my protest in no uncertain terms.

The Bible commands us that we should put serious effort into everything we do: 'Whatever things you do, do them with all your might.' I gulped in a great lungful of air and proceeded to obey this scriptural injunction by screaming blue murder at the very top of my voice. I think God must have heard me – certainly passing aliens picnicking on other planets probably heard my cries.

73

Now, in the slow motion that apparently precedes death, we continued our helpless spin towards the precipice. Oh dear.

Then I noticed that my friend, the driver, was not screaming – but rather, he was praying. Actually, he seemed to think that some dark skulduggery was afoot, because I heard him inform Satan in no uncertain terms to 'get off of the car'. I peered through the swirling windscreen, but there was no horned figure with pitchfork and red tights to be found perched on the bonnet. Still, praying seemed like a good idea, so I joined in – except that instead of a 'Bruce Willis – Intercessor' voice, what proceeded from my mouth sounded like Minnie Mouse with her tail caught in a lift door. And then the crevasse loomed, and so I decided to drop the prayer ministry and just get back to what I'm *really* good at – screaming.

The car tipped suddenly as we went over the side. What happened next defies logical explanation unless one concedes that there is a God who is interested in us. In a split second, the car was lifted up and shoved back onto the road. A lady driver who was coming down the pass stopped her car, so astonished was she at the sight. In a breathless roadside conversation with her a minute later, she told us that she saw three of our four wheels had gone over the edge – and then the car was lifted up. She was also a Christian, and was in no doubt as to the source of our roadside assistance.

To write these words presents me with a quandary: Christians – better Christians than I – die in car accidents. Just a couple of weeks ago, a young man with whom I have shared ministry fell asleep at the wheel and died instantly as he ploughed into a tree. He had made sacrificial choices to follow Jesus, and he had a bright, promising future for God ahead of him. But he was not spared.

I am tempted to never speak of the cliff-side rescue again. But to embrace that silence is to deny something that God definitely did. Perhaps, in order to affirm what God did do for me that day, I have to tiptoe into the realm of mystery. The fact is, I don't have a clue as to why I was spared when other more faithful friends of Jesus will die today in accidents around the world. But my half-knowledge must not prevent me from affirming that it did happen. God sometimes heals, and no disease is stronger that his muscle, but many are not healed.

That knowledge gives me a horror of the kind of Christianity that promises people sure results – health, healing, prosperity – as long as they follow a set of pre-packaged faith principles. Not only is God reduced to the status of a hapless vending machine, but also sincere people are hoodwinked. Faith is a love affair, and some-times an exasperating and confusing romance at that, rather than an easy climb up twenty solid stairs to suc-cess. Like any other relationship, it cannot be reduced to cold laws or clever formulas.

Did God bless you today? Good – then share the good news. But tread gently and sensitively around those who are currently living under a brass heaven, who still limp forward, painfully yet faithfully, waiting still for God. To affirm the power of a supernatural God in a world of pain and suffering is like being balanced precariously on a tightrope. It takes grace.

DECISIONS

WHERE TO NOW?

Guidance. It's a word that struck sheer terror, like a dagger to my heart, in my early years as a Christian. Things were going quite swimmingly until the day when someone mentioned something strange called 'The will of God'. Having worked out that this was not a document that listed heavenly bequests from God to his relatives, I set out on a painful trek to find this *will of God* for my life. Believers wiser than I advised me that I would need to seek *guidance*. Apparently, two navigational systems were on offer. The *'perfect'* will of God was the 'spot on, one hundred and eighty, bang on target' version available to the really keen. And there was something shady called the *'permissive'* will of God which the careless, slightly iffy apprentices of Jesus could walk in. I snorted with disdain: nothing less than the *perfect* version for me, I insisted. I wanted to be within the *perfect* will of God to the nearest yard – make that inch. I headed immediately for the local Christian bookshop in search of assistance in these weighty matters.

Unfortunately, there were lots of books about guidance on offer, which presented an immediate, paralysing dilemma. Which book about the will of God was it the will of God for me to buy? I wandered around the shop, and abstained from eating food for at least five minutes as I did, thinking that this miniature fast would bring revelation to my soul. Alas, I couldn't decide. Several book covers looked promising, but which was the right one?

I had heard that one should 'lay a fleece' whenever one is presented with a number of alternatives. Having worked out that I was not required to give birth to a sheep, I asked the Lord to cause the quiet, balding gentlemen who was the manager of the bookstore to drop kick me if I was selecting the wrong book. The said gentleman did not stir; I concluded that I was indeed on the right trail. He even flared his hairy nostrils as he rang up the till and wrapped my book: a sign, perhaps?

And so began a period of foggy confusion, as I sincerely wrestled with the issue of guidance. Some well meaning folks (who may have had previous employment counselling a bloke called Job) did their best to point me in the right direction. One of them said that God would speak to me if I just threw my Bible open at random. I had just started going out with Kay, who is now my wife, and was eager to know if she was a part of the perfect plan. Carefully removing all bookmarks, receipts and empty crisp wrappers from my Bible, I flipped it open, and stuck my finger at random on a verse. It was from Proverbs and warned me about consorting with prostitutes. I was horrified. Was there something that Kay wasn't telling me?

I'm not the first to trip over the Bible 'lucky dip' routine. It's an old chestnut, but worth telling in case you haven't heard it.

Man, desperate for guidance, throws open Bible and plonks finger on verse. It says, 'And Judas went and hanged himself.' Discouraged, he closed the Bible and decided to try Bible lucky dip again. The next verse he randomly found didn't help. It said 'Go thou and do likewise.' Feeling ever more desperate, he decided to give 'the divine dip' a final try. Throwing the Bible open one last time, he dramatically closed his eyes and stabbed his finger at the page. The verse said 'What you do, do quickly.'

Then I tried the practice of using everyday happenings – like the changing of traffic lights, for example – as 'if this happens, then that, that means this' indicators. Looking back, once again it seems like I must have been worthy of professional psychiatric care – but you'd be amazed how many people respond when, in public meetings, I ask how many have tried the 'traffic light guidance' routine. Nervous that the Lord might be calling me away from my apparently wanton girlfriend to a life of celibacy as a missionary to Africa, I offered myself to him while driving one day, and asked that, if he wanted me to don a pith helmet, that the next light would be green, for 'go'. Thankfully, the light turned red and I was spared a sweaty call to the Sahara. (OK. I confess. It was green, but I slowed down until it turned red). Yep, it was nuts.

Then I heard that you could tell if you were on the right track because you would feel peace – apparently this sense of peace would be like the umpire in a cricket match. A sense of unrest and emotional turbulence might indicate that the umpire was telling you that you were out for a duck – of the will of God, that is. This created some serious problems for me. Of course, I didn't have peace – mainly because I was terrified of making a mistake. It's like asking a trapeze artist if he feels peaceful, even as he senses that his foot is about to slide off the trapeze bar. *'So, as you face the possibility of falling headlong into oblivion below and meeting a rather crunchy end there – do you feel calm?'* I was locked in a circle of paralysis: I didn't have peace, because I didn't have peace, because I didn't have . . .

Then one day I decided to take a little look at that Bible verse and peace and the umpire, and found that it is talking about the need for harmonious relationships in the local church, and has nothing to do with guidance whatsoever. I felt somewhat angry about all of the unnecessary agonizing that I had gone through as a result of bad, out of context teaching. It just wasn't cricket.

But things were to get worse. Some bright spark suggested that finding the will of God was very easy – it was just the exact opposite of what *I* might want to do. It sounds crazy now, but it sounded perfectly reasonable back then. But it created emotional havoc. For example, what was I to do about Kay? I was obviously going out with her because I liked her and thought her attractive. So, that must be a no-no. I must surely find someone that I find numbingly boring and totally unattractive. Yes, that's it, I shall marry someone seriously ugly for your name's sake, oh Lord! Hallelujah! That'll crucify the flesh all right! (Some of you who have seen my photo are already concluding that she also got a hold of this mad idea.)

There are quite a few brands of this fairly twisted teaching in evidence. I've heard more than a few preachers harass congregations with the 'God's dreaming up something nasty for you' approach to guidance. 'Don't ever say that you don't want to do something. God has a way of making you do that very thing! I heard of a chap who hated curry with all of his heart, and wept at the possibility of ever having to go to a hot climate. But . . . (pause for effect and build atmosphere to maximum glee for the poor sweating unfortunate who is now spending his life doing what he hates doing in a place that he despises and where he hasn't had a square meal in years) guess what he's doing now for the Lord? Yes! He's a missionary in Calcutta!'

Of course there are times when God will ask us to do something that we're not that keen on: martyrdom, for example. But the notion that he is waiting to basically pour scorn on anything that I might like is, at best, somewhat perverse. Imagine me taking a similar attitude to Christmas present buying.

'Aha! Despite the fact that I know that my son would love a surfboard for a Yuletide gift, I shall hereby test his affection for me by purchasing some Carmen heated hair rollers. Yes!'

I also struggled with the idea that, as one writer says, 'God's will affects everything'. Even if that is true, which I doubt, then I took that to mean that there were to be instructions about every detail of life. Should I wear a green sweater, or my favourite blue one, and shop at Tesco, or Sainsburys? And if I played Cluedo at Christmas, was it already predetermined that Colonel Mustard did the murder in the study with the lead piping? Did God already know the result of a harmless game of table tennis – and more importantly, had he already decided who the winner should be?

I got into deeper philosophical hot water. I read one erudite chap, who declared, 'Would you like to know God's sovereign will for the past? Well, if something happened, it was part of the plan . . . ' Help! That means that two crazed schoolboys waving guns at Columbine High School, and summarily executing students and teachers before dispatching themselves was 'part of the plan'. It means that the screams and sobs of Sarah Payne, snatched and murdered by one of the most cold hearted people in history, was 'part of the plan'. And it means that the obscene photographs that captured the agony of those jumping out of the Twin Towers in New York to escape the furnace within was 'part of the plan'. I do not and will not believe that. I got myself into a right straightjacket about the whole business. And then one day it dawned on me: it was not the will of God that I be obsessed with the will of God.

God isn't just in the life-planning and direction business, moving his children around like pawns on a chessboard. And spirituality isn't about a kind of 'Mystic Megism' that seeks to continually download driving instructions from the beyond. Guidance, when it does come, flows out of friendship and relationship. God will just not be reduced to being an impersonal oracle: he will be, and ever is, Father.

And there are times when he seems to give us the chance to decide. There came a day when I got quite a shock. I genuinely asked for God's directive about a situation, and his clear reply stunned me. 'I don't mind. What do you want to do?' This certainly flew in the face of my belief that anything that I wanted was automatically *not* what God wanted. I'm not suggesting a 'just do what you want' approach across the board, but on that occasion, God stunned me by giving me a choice.

Twenty-five years later, I have something simple to say about guidance. Stop looking for the will of God. Read that again, because I meant what I said. Start looking for God. Enjoy him, love him, share your life with him, and let him know that you want what he wants.

Then guidance, when it is needed, will flow naturally, and you won't get into the charismatic neurosis that dogged my early years. You won't be always hunting for revelation – but true wisdom will find its place in your life.

And if anyone is looking for a pith helmet, I have one for sale. I've just seen another red traffic light.

SIN FOR DUMMIES

I don't get along too well with computers. I am currently the proud owner of an 'IBM Beelzebub' with a 666-megahertz chip. It is truly a servant of Satan, sabotaging my quiet, sanctified persona. I use it to tap out my sermons, but it always freezes up on me when I'm typing my third point about patience, and all my warm thoughts evaporate as I scream out loud and bite the screen.

Some of its occultic behaviour is probably due to the fact that I have input some things into it that were inappropriate – like a pint of lager, for instance. Tapping away late one night, I elbowed a glass of probably the worst lubricant for computers in the world, right into the keyboard. The sticky concoction gummed up the keys, and the computer itself seemed to have a silly smile for weeks. People thought that I had developed an on-line stutter as I sent e-mails with hhhhhhhello at the beginning.

Then there was the time I was just completing a PowerPoint presentation on the laptop, when the phone rang. I reached out to answer it, knocked a boiling kettle over, and reduced the computer to a steaming ruin in a second. The computer actually screamed – honest – and I joined in sympathetically. Another trip to computer hospital, this time with a scalded, outraged machine.

But my worst experience to date was the time when I accidentally formatted my hard drive. I should explain this highly technical term (!) to those blessedly uninitiated in such deep techno-secrets. Formatting your drive is the equivalent of taking the top of your head off, removing your brain, discarding said brain forever, and then replacing aforementioned skull cap. You wipe out everything in a flash.

I don't know why I did it. I was very tired, pressed the wrong series of command keys, and instructed the computer to format. This would mean the destruction of every sermon ever written, the wiping out of five years of accounts, and the nuking of my diary for the next two years. The computer itself raised a perturbed eyebrow at my instruction, and asked for confirmation of this unusual and indeed suicidal command. This was kamikaze behaviour. A warning message flashed on the screen, demanding confirmation of my intention to self-destruct.

'ARE YOU SURE?'

Of course I was sure, how dare you question my choices, oh evil, pathetic machine! In a moment of unbridled insanity, my finger hovered over the 'Y' key – again for the non-techno types, Y stands for 'yes'. I punched the key with attitude. And in a second or two, everything was wiped out. Even as I held the Y key down ever so momentarily, I realized the utter folly of what I had done. The hard disk was now empty. There was no way back, everything was history, but unrecoverable history. My reaction was, shall we say, not good. I wish I could tell you that I faced my foolishness with calm demure, murmuring, 'The Lord has given, and the Lord has taken away – blessed be the name . . . '

'Noooooooooooooooooo!' I screamed falsetto, and ran around the room at speed, bumping into furniture as I sprinted.

If only I had heeded the cautionary warning – *Are you sure?* – and had stopped for just a moment to consider my actions. I would have saved myself months of grief.

Instead, my impatient, unthinking haste destroyed everything.

And sometimes the same is true when it comes to a heady moment of temptation. In the heat of the moment, we find ourselves charging at a rate of knots down the mad pathway towards sin – and it is like a temporary madness. Casting aside everything that we know to be true, ignoring every Bible verse memorised, and every lesson of life learned, we leap headlong from a twilight zone of half consciousness into wrongdoing. If only there was an error message that automatically appeared before our eyes – 'Are you sure?' Or one of those time delay devices that they use in banks: the safe that's full of cash will not open for thirty minutes. This donkey brained human being who is currently being led more by his loins than his brain will not be able to sin for a full half hour: please wait and consider.

How many marriages might have been saved if the would-be adulterers had taken just a few seconds to ponder the faces of their children, or remember wedding promises made with such love and confidence, instead of just leaping thoughtlessly into a bed of roses and then thorns? Once there, nothing can ever quite be the same again.

How many lives might have been different if thoughtful, considered choices had been made, perhaps without the blurring that too much alcohol brings? How many children mowed down by drunk drivers would still be alive and laughing, if only there had been a pause before that extra pint? How many friendships might have been spared destruction if barbed words had been held back in time for the brain to catch up with the mouth?

So next time you're tempted to make a crazy, compulsive leap, stop and think for a moment. It could save you days – or even a lifetime – of regrets.

Are you sure?

THE EXTRA MILE

The late afternoon sun was wonderfully warm on our backs as we filed through the turnstiles, our day at Colorado's *Water World* at an end, or so we thought. We'd screamed, slid and splashed our way down dozens of chutes and raft rides, and now our bodies ached with the pleasant feeling of tiredness that tops off a good day of fun.

We picked our way through the hundred of cars. Our vehicle was easy to spot, loaded down as it was with all our bags and suitcases. This was an extended trip, and although our car had no kitchen sink within it, we did seem to have a lot of stuff. As we approached the car, my feeling of sleepy peace was suddenly shattered, as was the driver's window of our car. We had been robbed. Out of a sea of hundreds, perhaps thousands of cars, ours had been selected. Glass littered the concrete. My heart sank like lead.

Tearfully, frantically, we checked our bags to see what had been stolen. Most things were intact. A laptop computer, which I had foolishly left sitting on the back seat had been ignored: perhaps the thieves had been disturbed and had beat a hasty retreat. But there was a crucial item missing: a bag that contained Kay's jewellery, together with our passports, and the valuable resident alien cards (called green cards, even though they're blue) that are proof that we are entitled to live in America. Our airline tickets were gone too. Obviously, without passports, we would not be able to return to the UK. We would have to fly to Los Angeles to the British Embassy there to get them replaced, and then on to Portland, Oregon to get replacement alien cards at the American Immigration Building there. All of this would have to be done in the next day or two, and would cost us thousands in airfares. We were devastated.

Kelly stamped around the car park, hoping that maybe she would find that the passports had been discarded by the fleeing robbers, without success. Richard got on the phone to the police, and Kay wept with frustration: this was going to totally destroy our holiday. And for one rare moment in my life, I didn't panic, but felt a rush of inspiration and faith. Understand, dear reader, this is a rarity for me. Kay usually has the responsibility to be calm in a crisis and filled with faith. In the partnership that is ours, I usually accept the role of panic-stricken, uptight and agitated reactor, a role that I play with ease – it comes very naturally to me. But on this occasion – loath as I am to admit it in case you think me smug – I didn't feel panic at all, but sensed that all was going to be well. I gathered the family around and made an announcement that must have seemed like insanity.

'I think we should pray that we will get this stuff back in the next twenty-four hours', I announced, the wildness of the statement beginning to dawn on me even as it came out of my mouth. 'Let's ask God to help us – he can do it.'

I don't know if it was just wishful thinking, or a genuine gift of faith, but I said it anyway, and, right there in the car park, our feet crunching on the broken glass, we put our request in to God. 'Please get our stuff back.'

The police arrived, took our details, and told us that hell was likely to freeze over before we got our stuff back. Passports were very saleable, and anyway, mused the officer, 'Those thieves will be miles away from here by now.' We were advised to plan a trip to the West Coast to replace the stolen documents – and be quick about it. We drove to our hotel, the wind blasting now through the shattered window. A quick call to the British Embassy, answered by an official who had a Masters degree in blatant unhelpfulness, confirmed our fears. We would, all four of us, have to make the journey. But we had prayed, and so we decided not to allow the fun that had kissed the early part of the day to be stolen along with the passports. And we did have a wonderful evening together.

The next morning, we decided to go to the airport to report the loss of our tickets. The ticket clerk tapped away on her keyboard for a minute or two, and then everything changed; the sun came out from behind the clouds as she spoke.

'I have good news for you. Your passports, alien cards and air tickets have been found. They were discovered in a bush by a passer-by yesterday. Here's his number – he's eager to meet you. Here, make the call now.'

Breathless with excitement, I called our Good Samaritan. Apparently, the thieves had dumped our document wallet some miles from the water park – in that, at least, the policeman had been right. The wallet could have lain at the side of a road or under a bush for years, or perhaps never have been discovered. But this knight in shining armour of ours had seen something sticking out under the bush at the back of his home, and, realizing just how important these documents were, he immediately went to work. He called the police to report the find, who casually told him that they would stop by in the next few days to pick the wallet up; they did not connect our reported loss with his reported find at all.

Impatient with that, he told the police not to bother – he would track us down himself. Finding a receipt from a hotel, he called there, only to be told that we had checked out days earlier. Undeterred, he called some friends of ours in Oregon – their card was in the wallet – but they had no idea where we were or how to contact us. He then realized that we were from England, found some UK phone numbers that we had written down and were in there too, and he began to systematically call these transatlantic numbers, in a desperate and diligent search to track us down. Finally, discovering the airline tickets, he called the airline and had them put a note into our computer reservation, so that when we checked in, we would receive the wonderful news. I drove across the city, thanking God all the way. We were to get everything back, except a couple of items of jewellery, within twenty-four hours.

But we did so because one man – who I don't think was a Christian – went the extra mile. He greeted us like long lost friends. We bought him dinner, a somewhat feeble attempt to express our thanks for the timely rescue operation that he had mounted. He didn't know us from a bar of soap, but had simply decided to go out of his way to be kind. As we parted with handshakes and hugs, we thanked God for answering our prayers – and doing so through a stranger's decision.

ETERNITY

THE MUGGING

It was a vicious attack, sudden and violent, that came, not from a physical assailant, but from a thought that kicked its way into my head with a ferocity that was totally paralysing. It was a mental mugging. The thought formed itself inside my brain in a millisecond, whispering what I had always felt was unthinkable.

I am bored with God. I am bored with being a Christian.

I was doing my best to mind my own business when it happened. The scene of the attack was unusual: it happened in the quiet, air-conditioned sterility of an airport executive lounge. I had settled myself into one of those little cubicles that busy people on the move use, where you can plug your computer in, make a dozen phone calls, or write a note to your children. I fired up my notebook and settled down to work on a sermon. The other cubicles were occupied, and the hum of phone calls to secretaries, deals being done, and the fuzzy roar of modems shaking hands with the Internet droned away.

My attention was distracted by a conversation being held at high volume by a very smartly dressed chap in the next booth. Perfect creases in his trousers, short collar undone and expensive silk tie loosened in the lets-get-down-to-business-then style, he looked every inch the bright, young high-flier. Apparently, he was closing an eight million dollar deal with a major corporation. He was excited, animated even, as he finalized the details.

95

I peered at him discreetly. He can't have been more than thirty, and here he was, wheeling and dealing and being a major player. He was significant. Important. Key. And *very* necessary.

And suddenly, I saw myself as totally the opposite of all of the above. I felt the crisis that comes when, as Christian leaders, we feel that we are condemned to always deal with the invisible, the intangible, the here-after. All around me were people who were trading in very tangible, touchable commodities. Here was I, labouring again over a sermon that may make abso-lutely no difference whatsoever, delivered to people who may simply see its presentation as a mere snack in their regular diet of evangelical entertainment. I suddenly felt very small, very unaccomplished, surrounded as I was in this airport lounge loaded with over-achievers.

The apparent madness of a life lived for the invisible swept over me, followed quickly by a breaking wave of guilt that I should even think such a thought. And then, the taste of that guilt itself tasted bitter. The crushing bur-den of always living under the shadow of oughts: I ought to pray more; I ought to be a better leader; I ought to be able to see a miracle or two; I ought; I ought . . . pushed me under like a drowning man. I was gasping for breath.

I was stunned that I could be mugged so very easily. I had managed to keep afloat when hearing of a friend developing a brain tumour recently. Who was I to get angry, when she stands resolutely in the arena of her pain, her husband bravely, unquestioningly at her side? What right does a spectator of their anguish have to get angry, when they choose to trust?

And I had bobbed along hopefully when faced with the boring bits of Christian leadership; gossiping Christians that you may well spend eternity avoiding; evangelical politics and power plays, smilingly, greasily manoeuvred in the name of God; the cynicism that comes when you have been around Christian leadership for a while. It all feels like a loss of innocence that might come to an avid theatre-goer who wanders backstage, and is confronted by the scenery, the props, the instruments of the illusion.

I know how we leaders can engineer atmosphere, control people under the guise of exhortation, preach one thing and live another. I had seen that the lift in the worship was more the fruit of a well-timed key change than a heavenly visitation. And I had hesitated a few times over the fence of familiarity: the challenge of holding onto fresh faith when God is your job, when you are paid to be pious. But I had negotiated my way through these thoughts with relative ease. And here I was, being rugby tackled by an overheard conversation of a young go-getter. Never mind that he was dealing in the temporary and I in the everlasting. That was just my point: I wanted something very much in the here and now.

I *did* learn that God does seem to keep trekking with us when we want to quit on him. That weakness is often the landing strip that he looks for. When I finally got home, tiredness was a leaden thing draped heavily over me. I arrived at our empty house, dumped my bags in the hallway, and glared at the Everest of mail – a combination of bills and junk. The place smelt musty, and was cold. The dog didn't even greet me: my tired eyes told him that man's best friend wasn't going to get too much fuss today.

Within twenty-four hours, I would be climbing aboard another flight to speak about God to yet another group of hopeful people who anticipated some words from the Creator of Universe through exhausted, irritable me.

I didn't want to be there. I had no desire to talk about God, life, love, church, or indeed anything of any significance or weight. I wanted to crawl into bed for three days, waking only to watch a funny video or eat some unhealthy snacks. I didn't want to even give a passing thought to aspiration, commitment or discipleship, an old episode of *Father Ted* would do me just fine.

And for some reason that I just cannot figure, God helped, and some seriously significant things happened. I had been asked to speak about sex to a large youth celebration. Numbers of tearful young people, bruised by the abuse of 'Daddy's little secret', decided that enough was enough; it was time to blow the whistle. Just one of them would have made the whole weekend worthwhile.

And then, on the Sunday night, a young lady who hadn't passed through the doors of a church for five years, sat through the last twenty minutes of my talk, her shoulders shaking gently with tears as God met her. Numbers of people, eyes bright with gratitude, whispered their thanks, affirming that God had helped them and had used my bleary-eyed preaching to do so.

I'm not suggesting that my frantic scheduling is in any way commendable. It is the fruit of bad choices made a year ago, when a blank diary lay open before me. Only my own madness stained it with such hyperactivity.

But I have noticed that God seems to find weakness quite irresistible. When we are right at the end of our rope, it is then that he seems to delight in showing up.

So what of it all, a few days later? Well, I've figured out that I'm not actually bored with God. Who is more incredible, more colourful, more surprising than him? No, I am glad again that there is the sound of laughter at the heart of the universe, and that I know the source. What a marvel, that the creator is a friend.

But I think that being bored with life this side of fullness is normal. One day, all of us will see the face of

Jesus. Faith will be finished with, a discarded antique. Questions will be silenced by the breathtaking, crystal clear view. In the meantime, there may well be days when I'm too tired to believe, too weary to hope, and when a resolute, emotionless faithfulness to what is right is all that I know.

I'm really looking forward to that clear, heavenly view. Come on Jesus. Come on back.

THE SECOND COMING OF THE SECOND COMING

Twenty years ago, I had the Second Coming of Jesus all nicely sorted out, thanks to a helpful chart purchased from a bearded lady in the local Christian bookshop. The chart, with its ancient gothic typeface and its line drawings of the beasts and bowls of Revelation, gave me a pocket guide to the future of the Universe. Books with sensational titles advised me of the real, dark identity of Russia, the coming Chinese threat (more than an iffy takeaway), and the possible identity of the Antichrist.

Of course, the starring role of the aforementioned Beast changed around quite a bit. As I recall, Henry Kissinger did a brief stint, the current Pope was a perennial favourite, and even Bob Dylan held down the position for a while until he messed the whole thing up by professing, at least for a while, that he had been converted. This 'I'll name that beast in one' stuff continues to this day. Just this last Sunday, a lady told me that she had heard that a certain member of the British Royal Family was allegedly the latest candidate for the beasthood, as it were. I replied that this was a ridiculous and unfounded allegation: surely the beast wouldn't have ears that big . . .

The result of all this guesswork of twenty years ago was a sense that Jesus was possibly coming today, and that the odds of his returning were increased if you happened to be at the local cinema. God apparently wanted to combine the Second Advent with a super opportunity to catch out whole herds of popcorn-gripping believers having fun at the flicks. One would line up at the box office with one eye on the clouds above, and if someone slipped out of the smoky darkness and spent too long in the loo, panic would set in. Had they been swept into the vertical takeoff of the rapture, leaving their other movie loving pals behind? Great rejoicing – and great relief greeted the discovery that they had not been caught up in the air for the marriage supper of the lamb, but had merely been delayed by an unfortunate tummy upset.

I'm not sure why so many of us gave up on so much of that prescriptive eschatological stargazing. It's not that we consigned the Second Coming itself to the dustbin, although, to be frank, it was occasionally tempting. The 'Jesus might come today' stuff is no more sustainable on a long-term basis than 'I think we're on the edge of revival' rhetoric. You can't live on the brink interminably. After a while, it felt like we'd been waiting for the number 58 bus forever: in the end, you start to wonder if the bus will ever come. But we held onto the truth – and indeed, it is the truth – that Jesus will come again. We just quietly burned our charts, put away those 'evangelistic' movies which scared the living daylights out of people, and declared ourselves somewhat cornily to be 'pan-millennialists'. 'I used to be pre-millennial in my eschatology, but now I'm 'pan' – it'll all pan out in the end. Boom boom!

Some of us dumped our pocket guides to the future. But what did we put in their place, apart from a vague eschatological agnosticism?

Lately, the hirsute lady at the bookshop has been making a big comeback, particularly in America, where perhaps she was never out of vogue. Tim LaHaye's *Left Behind* series has been nothing less than a publishing phenomenon, with tens of millions of copies shifted.

Some dismiss these and other books as being Christian pulp fiction: science fiction eschatology not to be taken too seriously. But if we adhere to that view, then what's our understanding about all that material in Daniel and Revelation?

And all of this is not just about being theologically informed so that we can have lively chats about the Middle East at dinner parties. It is well known that President Bush is surrounded by wall-to-wall evangelical Christians, most of whom would take a view on biblical prophecy and the place of Israel. Never mind whether we agree or disagree with that view – the fact is that it is a very real likelihood that eschatology, far from being the plaything of seminary-bound academics who need to get out more, carries the potential of changing the world.

And in some circles, there is a very real fear of a 'Christian' Bin Laden rising up. Imagine a fanatical fundamentalist, who, taking the view that the temple must be rebuilt in Jerusalem if Jesus is to return, decided to give the Second Coming a little help by blowing up the Dome of the Rock . . .

So perhaps it's time for us to blow the dust off of our Bible commentaries and start to wrestle with the apocalyptic language of the Bible once more. Never mind what we *don't* believe – what *do* we believe?

HOMECOMING

Tyler was sixteen when he died. He had lived in the valley of the shadow of death since he was eight years old, although it was not until his final year on earth that he learned just how terribly ill he was. The battle for Tyler began when, at the tender age of four, he developed neurofibromatosis – a disease that turns the body into a harrowingly efficient production line for tumours. Many suffer from this disability and live to tell the tale, but Tyler was one of the one per cent for whom this is not so. In fact, his was the worst case that the doctors could recall. His body was a mass of small predators, which conspired together to steal his ability to walk, birthing a brain tumour and robbing him of his right eye when he was just eight. He would endure twelve major surgeries, and, in one six-week period, was unconscious beneath the scalpel for an unthinkable forty-nine hours. In the end, the doctors stopped counting tumours, and counted days left instead. They knew that it would not be long.

For fourteen years, life said a firm 'no' to Tyler. His desire to play his beloved baseball was rudely declined: instead, he rode an electric wheelchair. He worked for a while in a skateboard shop, and would have been delighted to ride the sleek board they presented to him, but any hope that he might have had of whiling away balmy days surfing around the sidewalks with friends was cruelly dashed. Like any teenager, he dearly wanted

103

to drive a car. But life's verdict has been firm, and without possibility of appeal: no. And his bike, which he had once been able to pedal furiously, was denied him too.

Unusually for one so young, Tyler's greatest ambition had been to become a father. Testament surely to the love of Josh and Sherri, his parents, Tyler longed to see his own children's laughing faces one day. When he was told that his disease was terminal, his first response surprised: 'I hope that I get to have kids first.' They said that, if he *did* live to become a dad, that his own offspring would have a fifty/fifty chance of being struck down by this terror disease. He determined that he would perhaps grow up to have one child, and adopt some more. But the prognosis was devastating, its cold accuracy correct – his hope of having children would never be. No.

And perhaps one of the toughest denials for the tactile Tyler was the fact that his family couldn't hug him anymore, a refusal born of kindness, not coldness, because to embrace him would have sent his nerves into searing agony. And he would watch longingly as Dad wrestled with his brothers and sisters; that rough-and-tumble playfulness way out of bounds for his fragile frame.

Despite all of the denials, Tyler was defiantly a 'Yes' person. His parents are quick to insist that he was no saint, and like us all, he had his moments where, like the rest of the human race, he could miss the mark. But for his disability, Sherri insists, he might have strolled into more trouble than he could navigate in a wheelchair. But there was gold produced in his furnace of pain as well. He determinedly pursued relationships, even when his telephone went quiet, as his school friends, not knowing what to say, how to act, stopped calling. He had a particular hankering to help a workmate who had a reputation for being a rough, tough guy, who had subsequently moved away. The night before he died, Tyler received a call from that long-distance friend, who insisted on coming to see him, and they spent an hour together that final evening.

Tyler said 'Yes' to what others saw as 'No' situations. When he was forced to abandon his regular bike, his dad took him and bought him a three-wheeled version in bright yellow. Depressed that his son would be reduced to an uncool three wheeler, Josh felt gloomy about the yellow machine, until Tyler blurted out on the way home: 'I am so blessed! I have got a three-wheeled bike!' No irony or sarcasm here, just gratitude, and celebration in the face of indignity. If his sight became dim, his humour stayed sharp. One night, as he sat with his family in the kitchen, all faces stained with tears, he announced that the 'Sob Fest', as he dubbed it, should come to an end. 'How about we all pack it in and go to bed?' he suggested. He gave Josh a ring with the single word 'Dad', printed on it, prompting yet more sobbing. Later, he held out his own hand, pretending that there was a ring there, and mimicked his father's crying with a grin.

They asked him if he would like to go on a dream trip, and, as many chronically ill children have done, he chose to go to Disney World. But there's a detail to note here: it was impossible for Tyler to go on a single ride; again, to do so would have bought waves of pain. His family knew that he had put in the request for their sake.

Sherri wanted to explain to her son that there was a bright future, out of this world, ahead. She compiled a book about his life, calling it 'Buckets of Glory'. The rationale was simple; she figured that her boy had been drenched with hundreds of buckets of suffering and pain. The Bible teaches that the glory out there will far outweigh and outshine any suffering down here. The maths is simple – there would be hundreds and hundreds of glory buckets waiting for her Tyler.

There was one other hope that Tyler had cherished. He had liked a girl in his church for a very long time. Erica is blonde and beautiful, with a warm, winning smile and a tender heart for God. In America, the football season begins with a so-called 'homecoming' party. Tyler asked Erica if she would do him the courtesy of accompanying him to this very special event. Somehow, the news of the proposed date got around the town. Two limousine companies called to offer the finest transport available, free of charge. A local florist provided the most beautiful bouquet to crown the evening. A jeweller gave an earring and necklace set for Tyler to present to his date – and three restaurants called to offer free dinner. But the big question remained: would Erica say 'Yes' to the date?

Tyler returned home from the hospital, to discover that his front garden had been totally transformed. Erica's family had pitched in to create a garden-wide carnival of colour. Bright balloons bounced in the breeze. Bunting garlanded the hedges. But what demanded Tyler's attention, as he stared, speechless, at the garden, was the dozens of fluorescent posters that had been placed everywhere. Many of them carried just one word, bold and arresting.

YES. YES. YES. YES.

Tyler, resplendent in his rented tuxedo and top hat, and the lovely Erica were transported to the party like royalty. He danced with her by flipping the joystick of his electric wheelchair backwards and forwards. It was a wonderful evening, when, just for once, life said a big 'Yes'.

And now, as you read this, Tyler is gone, his battle with the tumour machine that had been his body finally over. Sherri and Josh sensed that, as parents, they were about to witness what they saw as a real privilege – the entrance of their son into heaven. Three gifts were given to Tyler as he ended his life here. He had been completely deaf for five months, but, towards the end, he was able to hear the faintest whisper, the quiet reassurances of Mum and Dad as they prepared him for the great journey. And then, the night before he went, he reported hearing a voice, calling his name: a summons from above to the party? Finally, he was granted the gift of giving, even as he died. He was urgently insistent that his parents should not be alone when he died, and waited for help and support to come before he slipped peacefully away. And, as his family, including siblings Jeremy, Charlie, Katie and Colby gathered together, six of them to whisper their farewells for now, he deliberately went around the circle of them, pointing specifically at each one, and in sign language, using hands that he could barely move because of pain just the day before, he spelled out, 'I love you'. They whispered, 'We release you'. And as he flew away, they said that the sense of peace in the room was thick, tangible.

Something tells me that, when he skipped up the pathway to be with Jesus, the clumsy wheelchair an unnecessary accessory now, that the Lord himself wasn't the first sight he saw. Call me sentimental if you like. But, knowing Jesus, I reckon that Tyler had a special 'homecoming' party in heaven: a few billion bright buckets, brimming over with glory; a bike with two wheels, not three. And perhaps, to welcome him, there was a rash of a million bright posters on display, each one with just one word scrawled upon it.

'Yes'.

Tyler is home.

UNITY

OLD TREASURES

Watching people is one of my favourite hobbies. Give me a spare ten minutes and I'll happily park myself on a bench somewhere and just watch the teeming world go by. Fear not, it's not voyeurism. But I enjoy wondering about the lives of those nameless people as they drift by; who are they, and what are their hopes and their histories, their dreams. What are their stories? I look at the lines etched deep on their faces and wonder what circumstances drew those indentations. What laugh-out-loud moments of joy have been theirs? What jet-black days of hopelessness and despair have they navigated?

And where and what are they now? I know that, as they stroll by in silence, their brains are probably buzzing: tangible thoughts, must-do lists and mushy, shapeless feelings unquantified by words, are crackling around inside those strangers' heads. Sometimes their eyes betray just a hint of what is playing on the screen of their inner selves; the slightest wisp of pain, fear, pleasure, wistful thinking, wishful thinking. Did I read them correctly, I wonder? I will never know.

Just lately, I've been noticing older people. I've looked into the faces of hunched-over old ladies, their red-veined faces gouged deep where they have frowned, or smiled, or wept. Some of them are bright-eyed, young in heart and face, the adventure still in progress. And some are now being greatly betrayed by their bodies, hunched over by bowing spines, their walk a laboured crawl, their watery blue eyes glazed against the cold. Sprightly old gents pass me, all smart and blue-blazered, a regimental badge worn with pride on their pockets, some with cloth caps, clip-on ties and walking sticks with rubber ends. Blue-rinsed ladies, with headscarves and wicker shopping baskets and great, thick coats . . .

. . . And I've wondered just what on earth these seniors think about today's world – and my generation in particular. Just yesterday, a couple that looked like they'd been married for life crept slowly past my observatory bench. Just then, a gaggle of twelve-year-olds brushed into them roughly as they strode by, their loud, effing this and effing that banter staining the air. I saw the sad look in the old man's eyes: he sensed their disdain and total lack of respect. He shook his head in defeat and resignation, and a fear that should never be permitted was written all over his wife's face. Perhaps they had known more than enough terror, being old enough to have walked through a world war, or maybe two.

What must these veterans think of us? My generation has never known what it is to go to the railway station to wave goodbye to a uniformed husband or father and wonder if you will ever see him again. We have not known the endless grinding struggle of economic depression. Peering fearfully through our fingers during the bloody opening scenes of *Saving Private Ryan* has been the closest that we have known of the searing butchery of war. We have not seen the death of hope and sanity that comes when people are forced to hack the lives out of each other on a battlefield. And yet, mine is the generation of the great escape. We have dulled our miniature pressures with substance abuse or on the soft padding of the psychotherapist's couch. We have far more than they ever had, and we take it for granted too:

our toys, we feel, are our right. What do they think, who marched to defend what rights they had – but many of whom lost great chunks of their youth or their friends – what do they think of us?

My father was a prisoner of war for four years, his youth swallowed up when he was captured early in the war in the desert of North Africa. The years that were supposed to be footloose and fancy free were spent caged behind rolls of barbed wire. No Friday night laughter with mates at McDonalds; he became pale and gaunt on a near-starvation diet. But he would never tell me very much about the wartime years. I used to think that his was a generation unable to speak: they could tell you what they had done, but not what they felt. I think I was wrong. His was a generation who had glimpsed the unspeakable, and perhaps some of them could never fully feel anything again. To open the door on their innermost feelings would be too dangerous, and so they locked and bolted it and got on with the job of trying to be sane again – just by existing another day.

And sometimes the old feel estranged in our churches. For them, the music *is* too loud, the hymns that we have discarded have been anthems of strength and hope for their journey, yet we can dismiss those songs with a sneer and insist that they embrace *our* choices. Some of them are not so much stuck in the mud, they just are wearied by our change-is-here-to-stay obsessions, and in some cases, they have seen all our brilliant, 'new' ideas before, wrapped in other packaging, and they are not impressed.

So look again at that old boy whose nose and ears refused to stop growing, and whose eyes are misty with memories. Tread gently around the widow who has lost her friend, companion and lover of sixty years: do not slap her with 'He had a good innings'. For her, the game

ended far too quickly. Put the word 'codger' away, and
stifle your giggles when Doris asks if we can please sing
that hymn, just once, next Sunday. Week in, week out,
she tries her best to get in step with *our* rhythm, hideous
though it sounds to her.

Are there irritating, crotchety, stubborn seniors about?
To be sure. But look again past fluffy hats and flowery
frocks; past well-worn checked jackets and dribbling
noses; past silvery hairstyles and ties worn for shopping.
There are treasures to be found in old vessels, and they
won't be here forever.

RAW FELLOWSHIP

It was twenty-five years ago. I was a fresh-faced theological student, ready to change the world for Jesus by next Tuesday. I was keen, to say the least. I could bellow, 'Praise the Lord' during worship times with a cannon-like gusto, causing other, more contemplative worshippers to cardiac arrest. I was always armed to the teeth with dog-eared tracts, and with a spring-loaded pocket Bible ready to draw at lightning speed and pistol-whip unsuspecting pagans. And I assumed that *my* church was the *best* church. I viewed people from other churches affectionately; compassionately even, feeling sympathy for those who had not had the opportunity to hear about *our* church. It was, surely, the pinnacle of the body of Christ worldwide. If only we could get the BBC cameras in to our place – then all the inhabitants of planet earth would convert at the sight of it. Or so I surmised.

One Saturday afternoon, I was not feeling led (or inclined) to assault innocent shoppers with ageing Christian literature. I decided to visit the local council-run leisure centre, a respectable establishment, and have a sauna. Checking carefully that it was indeed a session reserved for men only, I paid my money to a very attractive young lady at the entrance who gave me my change and handed me a towel. The sauna was quiet, so I jumped visibly when a thirty-stone naked man shot out of one of the cabins and hurled his massive girth straight into an icy pool. There was just about an inch of water encircling him. His plunge into the freezing water was a miracle of precision engineering, self-targeting missile that he was.

Everyone was naked except for white towels folded perilously around their mostly expansive waists. I stripped off, and stepped under one of the protruding, fizzing heads in a white tiled open shower area. All was going rather well, when suddenly my vigorous soaping was interrupted by a voice from behind me. As I turned round quickly, I realised – too late – that it was in fact a female voice. It was the blonde lady with the ministry in towel distribution who I had met at the entrance – and now, she had stopped by for a chat.

'Hello, love, first time here is it?' she said, looking me straight in the eye, which caused me to be thankful. I replied that I was indeed a newcomer – my whole body now rapidly turning a blotchy, embarrassed shade of red. Rats. I had no gospel tract with which to recover my modesty, no pocket New Testament – indeed, no pocket.

'Where are you from then?' she replied, as if it was absolutely normal to pass the time of day with a naked chap who you've never met before – as indeed, for her, it was.

'I'm from the Bible College down the road', I testified truthfully, the surreal nature of this conversation now beginning to really hit me. But surreal was about to get utterly bizarre.

'Oh, great', she replied with bright eyes. 'I go to a little brethren chapel round the corner.'

Suddenly I noticed a little gold cross on the lapel of her uniform. For just a moment, I forgot that I was without trousers, and was tempted to ask her about the ecclesiology and governmental system of her particular fellowship. '*So, how does a church with a plurality of elder-ship rather than a defined ministerial leader actually function?' 'And were the closed brethren becoming more open?'* And then I realized that I was being one of the most open brothers in the history of the church, being minus my kit. But she didn't bat an eyelid. Apparently, she was not only a distributor of towels, but also a retriever of them. She would meander through the sauna collecting discarded towelling, and chatting with the guys as she went. They had become quite used to her, and regarded their own state of undress with the same carefree spirit that one enjoys in the presence of the medical profession currently.

But I couldn't contain my embarrassment, my body now so blushing red that I looked like a traffic light. I mumbled 'God bless you' and turned back to face the white tiled wall. A brotherly handshake didn't seem appropriate.

I've never been back to that leisure centre. But I did do my bit for interdenominational unity and understanding . . . naked.

IN-FLIGHT STUFF

FEAR OF FLYING

It had not been a good flight at all. Cooped up for eleven long hours, some passengers were fighting boredom by pondering their lunch trays and playing 'Name that Food'. Most guessed wrongly; the fodder looked like an aerial view of a farmyard. It was so inedible and unattractively presented that some speculated that the airline employed an ex-wrestler to beat up the nosh just prior to serving. The toilet was so small that one needed training as a contortionist to sit down, and once seated, there was a real fear that one might remain wedged in that position while trans-navigating entire continents. I wanted to get off the plane. Now.

I shifted uncomfortably in my seat, hemmed in as I was by two bodies. An evangelist friend was seated to my left, and to my right there sat a lady who was certainly no frequent flier. She was afraid. Very afraid. I'd like you to think that I knew of her fear because I 'sensed it in my spirit', as they say. Alas, this was no feat of discernment. She was eating the in-flight magazine, which gave me a hint. Her tension was palpable, fingers knotting and unknotting repeatedly, sideways glances out of the window every few seconds. My evangelistic colleague had also noticed her terror. He jabbed me in the ribs, and hissed urgently in my ear.

'Lucas! Look – the lady next to you is obviously terrified of flying.'

I nodded dumbly. He was so right. But what should I do about it?

The Billy Graham wannabee to my left hissed again. 'Why don't you offer to pray for her? Fear of flying is no fun you know. She needs your help.'

He was right, of course. But I was tired, bored, uninspired, and somewhat beset by the temporary atheism that attacks Christian leaders when they have to sit doing nothing for too long. We carried on flying.

Then we hit a patch of turbulence, or so Nigel the pilot informed us (all pilots are called Nigel, it's a requirement of their training). The so-called 'patch' so threw the plane around that I felt like underwear in a washing machine. The bump created an instant reaction in our row of seats. The evangelist to my left shouted in tongues for an urgent second or two. My friend was helped by the tongues speaking, and so was a Turkish man two seats down who thought that someone was helpfully sharing a recipe in his dialect. I repented of my atheism in a second. And the terrified lady passenger screamed and began eyeing up the seat in front of her as a potential snack, her magazine now in shreds.

Hiss and jab from the left. 'Did you hear that, Lucas? The lady screamed.'

Yes, I know, Sherlock, it was in my ear that she did holler.

'And look . . . she's crying now . . . aaahhhh . . . have you no heart? Pray for her!'

Right. Pray for her. She's going to think that this is the most creative chat-up line of her life. 'Ello, darlin, ow about I pray for you then?'

We carried on flying. And then we apparently skimmed over the top of Mount Everest – or *major* turbulence according to Nigel up front. That was it. The poor lady screamed again, reached out and grabbed my hand, and wouldn't let go. We sat there for a few seconds, she and I, total strangers, hand in hand now. Time for a jaunty skip down the aisle of the plane, perhaps?

A third jab and hiss. 'Do something, Lucas! That woman is in trauma . . . why . . . she's holding your hand!'

I know. It's my hand. Why don't you go and do some door-to-door work on the emergency exit?

I whispered to my friend that I had now definitely done my bit, in my ongoing ministry of holding hands. Why didn't he offer to pray for her? He leaned over me, and spoke to her kindly.

'Excuse me, madam. I notice that you don't like flying. Well, my friend and I – he whose hand you are currently gripping – are both Christians. Would you like us to say a prayer for you?'

I braced myself for the hysterical laughter, the mocking disdain, and the recognition that I was holding hands with the President of the World Humanist League. But no rejection came at all. Her face, so creased with anxiety, relaxed into a nervous smile. She spoke.

'Pray? Oh, that would be lovely. Please do – I'm so grateful.'

I was stunned. I had anticipated a negative response from her, and so had failed to speak at all. My friend's offer of prayer was actually exactly what she had been waiting for. She was most grateful.

How often do we project our fears of rejection onto those who have not heard the good news yet? We anticipate a frosty response and so, fearful of the embarrassment that might result, we clam up, walk on by, and miss an opportunity for kindness. We pass up the chance to offer a cup of cold water in Jesus' name, fearing that the thirsty will spit it out with a curse. We keep on flying, as it were. And leaders can do this with their congregations, nervous about introducing change, because they see a negative response as almost inevitable. Leaders can spend their whole lives shadow boxing. But it isn't always like that. The lady in seat 31b smiled softly for the rest of the trip, and thanked us again – my friend for his prayers, and me for the loan of my hand – at the end of the flight. Which is even more surprising, when you consider how my friend prayed. No quiet, sensitive, *'Father please help this dear lady'* gentle touch from him. He jumped into a major full-on intercession at the top of his voice.

'Oh God, deal with this turbulence, and calm this lady's fears, RIGHT NOW, in Jesus' name, we command it, WE PROCLAIM IT.'

He was loud, passionate, and pebbledashed the left-hand side of my face with spit. All of the other passengers looked around, eager to know the source of the 'disturbance' and looked at me. They were embarrassed. I was embarrassed.

But the lady was unfazed by the wrestlemania prayer. She just smiled, and nodded, and smiled again. And I think God laughed.

THE POWER OF REPUTATION

'Oh my goodness, you're not, are you?'

I sighed as yet another friend's eyebrows shot into vertical takeoff, their mouth agape in horror. What was the reason for their stunned reaction? Had I announced a transsexual trip into women's ministry as a sister called Mandy? Had I just revealed that I have used my life of Christian leadership as a cover for my real employment as a member of a Colombian drug cartel? No, the shocked response was ignited because I revealed that Kay and I were planning to take a holiday in Tenerife.

Based on the comments that I had heard, our air flight and brief sojourn in Tenerife would surely be a nightmare. I anticipated boarding a winged cowshed supervised by flight attendants who would help passengers into their seats with the assistance of a high voltage cattle prod. In fact, when we boarded the plane, it was to a smiling welcome with classical music playing in the background. I was expecting them to pump "Ere we go, 'ere we go, 'ere we go' at high volume through the PA system.

It's true that the seats were a little snug: actually, they were designed to haul teams of limbo dancing leprechauns around the world. And the Adams family was seated behind me. A junior Adams (whose first name was surely Damien) kept pulling the seat back and then allowing it to cannon forward into the back of my head.

I ended up suffering from whiplash, and Damien nearly became an infant skydiver. But that JMC flight was really quite pleasant (JMC apparently doesn't stand for Just Might Crash), and the food was far superior to the transatlantic swill I've been served lately. The reputation of charter flights is undeserved.

As for Tenerife itself, I had been led to believe that I would surely bump into rampaging hordes of lager assisted gentlemen, all bedecked in Union Jack shorts, with grubby, knotted handkerchiefs on their heads. They would all surely be sporting lobster-coloured beer bellies seven times the size of their heads. All females would be wearing 'Kiss Me Quick' hats and would remove their bras at any and every opportunity, even in the event of an unexpected freeze. Again, this was not so. I did spot one lady attired in a T-shirt that advised us that 'Some Girls Do, Some Girls Don't, and I Just Might'. Admittedly, this is not likely to be a quote from the book of Proverbs, and was almost certainly not purchased from a Christian bookshop, but it was the only naff uniform in sight. And while there were a few ladies who were into bare and indeed pendulous fashion, most, thankfully, kept their tops on. And Tenerife has its beauty spots as well as the fish and chip promenades. I *did* meet a few chaps wandering around with gold hoops the size of juggling rings inserted in their voluminous abdomens, but they really were a minority.

The truth is that Tenerife, and budget airlines, tend to suffer because of image and reputation. And often, the reality doesn't correspond to the reputation at all, but locations, businesses and individuals suffer because they have at some time been tarred with the brush of generalization. This often happens in the church, where we of all people should believe in the possibility that a person can grow and change, quite simply because of God. But instead, we can box people up in a coffin of stereotype, chaining them to their history, dooming them to be victims of negative reputation.

A positive reputation also carries its own dangers. I have come to believe that one of the worst things that a church can gain is profile and attention – and the reputation that comes as a result. Reputation is usually based on history (so by the time that word gets out, everything may have changed) and is usually fuelled by rumour and exaggeration (not only are some reputations wide of the truth – they *never* were accurate). But the true power of reputation is its ability to take a church into the pea soup fog of self-deception. We start to believe our own press releases. Prophets come among us, sniff a sense of what used to be, and tell us that we are wonderful. Thus, we continue to believe the fairy tale. Surely, if everyone else thinks we're doing so well – God included – then we cannot fail?

The church at Laodicea had a reputation – and with a few well-chosen, acerbic words, Jesus drove a truck right through it. 'I am rich; I have acquired wealth and do not need a thing' was the spin. Jesus had another view. They were poor, blind and naked.

So let's beware the power of reputation. Whatever your image, ask the God of 20/20 vision for his verdict. And be careful about writing people off because of yesterday's mistakes. If I read my Bible correctly, the only kind of reputation that we really need to be concerned with is how we're perceived by those who are *not* followers of Jesus; and, of course, by Jesus himself.

Meanwhile, Damien, the demonised toddler, who has gifted me with whiplash, might really be a nice child at heart. And he might be in need of a parachute . . .

GRACE ABUSERS

I stood in the airport check-in line, dark clouds gathering in my heart as I waited. And waited. The prospect of yet another transatlantic flight spent with my legs wrapped around my neck for nine hours filled me with dread. I just wanted to be home. Airports are such lonely places, emotional black holes that are crammed full of people who have no desire to be there at all; they just desperately want to get home / on holiday / to the business meeting. And the notion that air travel is glamorous couldn't be more flawed: sitting strapped inside a silver tube with three hundred travellers, most of whom are fighting a losing battle against high altitude flatulence is hardly enchanting. I stepped forward to the ticket counter, and wished that 'beam me up Scotty' was a usable prayer that could just get me home, *right now*.

In a second, the sun came bursting out behind the dark clouds, as the check-in agent spoke.

'Good morning Mr Lucas. I have good news – you've been upgraded to business class today.'

I wanted to kiss her. Indeed, I wanted to kiss everyone in the airport, dance a waltz, sing an excerpt from The *Sound of Music*, and laugh out loud over the airport PA system. Business Class! A big, comfy seat, all to myself, with champagne and edible food that looks and even tastes like food and flight attendants who smile and don't walk up and down the aisle glaring like sentries on patrol and . . .

... This was going to be beautiful. Like a stunned lottery winner, I offered my grateful thanks, and headed for the airport lounge, my heart dancing with heady exhilaration. Suddenly, the airport was a truly beautiful place to be, filled with lovely, friendly people – or so it seemed. The receptionist in the lounge smiled, and asked me why I was so happy. Breathlessly, I told her my news – I had been upgraded!

I chatted with the receptionist for around fifteen minutes, and she told me some strange news – that many passengers react weirdly when they get a free upgrade. One would think that everyone would be brimming with gratitude – upgrading is like the airline is giving you a cheque for a couple of thousand pounds, such is the difference between the ticket cost of flying coach and business. And yet, strangely, many people become haughty and aggressive when they discover that they are sitting in a better seat. They become loud, demanding, and obnoxious – and some even threaten to report the person who has upgraded them! They abuse the grace that has been showered upon them, and attack the very people who have shown them kindness.

I wondered if I have been a grace abuser. I have been freely, outrageously forgiven – but how willing am I to pass that grace around to those who irritate and offend me? Through the cross, God has granted me the ultimate upgrade – from a lost forever to an eternity loaded with the genuine luxury of closeness to Jesus.

I have encountered too many churches that have been ripped apart by people who know well how to sing 'Amazing Grace', but they themselves are graceless, emotionally shrivelled and mean. Experts in conflict resolution say that Christians can be the worst at dealing with disagreement. Perhaps that's because of our insistence that we drag God into every conflict and discord, demanding that he agree with *our* preference and opinion. Slogans and clichés abound when we fall out – we're not just irritated with each other, we're 'grieved in our spirit'. It's not just that the music on Sunday wasn't to our taste – suddenly, God himself must have put his hands over his ears: after all, *we* didn't like it – so surely *he* didn't.

Throw in a bucketful of emotive prophesies, and a liberal sprinkling of spiritual superiority and you've got a recipe for total disaster.

The Bible is patently clear about our need to not just enjoy and receive grace, but to pass it around. The forgiven are commanded to forgive; we who must drive heaven to distraction with our idiotic, bumbling sinfulness are exhorted to put up with each other's foibles. We are objects of love, children of a God who is willing to trust us with everything, including the redemption of a planet. That should lead us to run from cynicism and to genuinely believe the best of each other. We will of course be disappointed. Far better that though, than to live a jaundiced existence, empty of hope or optimism.

Meanwhile, back in the airport lounge, another surprise was in store. Just five minutes before the flight, the friendly receptionist hurried up to me. With a huge smile, she whispered: 'I know you've already been bumped up to Business Class, but we need to move another passenger up – so I'm *double* upgrading you, and putting you in First Class today. That means you get to sleep in a real bed, and you get the best food available.'

My jaw almost hit the floor. Grace upon grace! The first class seat would cost ten times the price of my ticket. I asked her why she had done it.

'It's simple. You were nice to me. Have a great flight.'

IN PRAISE OF DOUBT

Doubt. It's surely the herpes of evangelicalism. People talk about it in hushed tones; they worry that it might be contagious, and fear that their reputation will be damaged irreparably if anyone knows that they've got it. And it's very boring when an outbreak hits you. For me, doubt usually comes when I'm in an atmosphere of great certainty, like one of those boisterous celebration meetings where, if you're careful, you can end up with a nasal rebore from a low-flying flag. You know the feeling – the bloke next to you is head-butting a tambourine with a monotonous rhythm that is causing you to have fantasies about killing him. The lady sitting in front of you is so ecstatic about being a Christian that she has had her hands raised high in the air in praise throughout the whole meeting, including during twenty minutes of numbing notices. The cheery Red Coat-type leader on the platform is gushing breathy platitudes into the microphone: 'Don't you feel the Lord in this place. He is here!' The woman in front of you stretches out and positively touches the ceiling with her worshipping fingernails, the bloke next to you is gnawing his tambourine now with a rabid enthusiasm, and you sigh, crushed for the moment by the burden of believing. Is all this God-stuff true? Is anyone out there beyond the canvas of this tent / plaster of this ceiling?

The other time when I get mugged by doubt is when flying. Actually, I am seated right now in the innards of

131

a rather large British Airways jet, which is aimed at America. I shall shortly be dispensing large chunks of biblical teaching to some assorted gatherings of rather nice Christian people. I am, right now, hurtling through the sky at 500 mph, my trajectory carefully navigated by computers, enabling Nigel the pilot to announce the time of our projected touchdown to within a minute or two, even though we are still three thousand miles from our destination.

But the laws of physics and the precision genius of computer chips do not govern my emotional and spiritual condition. At this moment, I feel less certain about my own ability to do anything useful for Jesus. I'm not sure who I doubt more – him or me. Today, while wrestling with a rather bland chicken Caesar salad at 36,000 feet, I found myself looking around the cabin and becoming increasingly unsettled about my faith, just as a result of surveying the backs of the heads of my fellow passengers. What is it that they do to cause this spiritual nervous tick to erupt in me? Simple. They unnerve me because of their *normality*. They sit and nurse their plastic cups and appear to have no concerns about holiness or morality, about the meaning and purpose of life or the life-exploding eruption that breaks upon a soul when it discovers that there is a Creator alive and well at the heart of the universe – and one who knows *me*. I see no signs of fretfulness on their faces because of the niggling impotence of the church that professes Christ's name so boldly, but witnesses to his life so pathetically. No, they just sit there, living another day without apparent depth or significance, mesmerized by just existing, and for a moment, I envy them, and feel that to believe all of the time is too much like hard work. And then I begin to really worry about myself in my secret, scandalous envy. My jealousy is truly wicked. Why, I am carrying in my bag a black, leather-bound book that apparently announces that these people are lost, and are themselves tiptoeing inch by inch into the black hole of a lost eternity. I berate myself: do I believe this enough to do something about it? Am I truly convinced that these nice, pleasant people, who apparently were made from a different gene pool from the serial killers and concentration camp guards of this earth are really so lost? Round and round the confused, fearful thoughts tumble, and for a while I feel more lost than they. And some of them shake their plastic cups with annoyance, because their ice is melting. And I shake my head in vain, hoping to dispel some of the ether inside my skull, but it persists, and, for a good while, God seems a long way off at 36,000 feet up. The plane zooms effortlessly forward, a precision dart on course for its destination. But the cabin seems filled with fog as I reach for my laptop and begin to write this chapter. A few moments of reflection will cause me to know that, actually, to live life for nothing, to merely survive, is no blessing, but a true curse. But in a tired, and the even mildly depressed condition that long plane flights seems to create in me, I feel battered by waves of uncertainty and disorientation.

Doubt. Well, there's no magic conclusion here, no slick recipe to banish doubt for good. Just the realization that we all suffer from it once in a while. One day, we'll see Jesus, face to face, and life in the twilight zone of believing will be over – forever. In the meantime, we live on the spiritual dark side of the moon, his face sometimes made distant and blurred by flesh, by life, by busyness, by fear. Resurrection will bring face-to-face revelation, and what a joy that will be. In the meantime, if you sometimes doubt, it doesn't make you a 'C' grade Christian, or a mighty pagan.

It just means that you're not dead yet.

PARENTING

A DRIVING LESSON

Teaching your children to drive is not a good idea. Let me rephrase that. There should be a clear biblical command prohibiting such madness, sternly advising would-be parent driving instructors that they shall be hereby stoned to death if they attempt filial driving tuition. Maybe there is a verse about this buried in the ox's gall bladders of Leviticus: 'Rideth not in thine daughter's chariot or sudden filthy great boils shall break out all over thine head' or something similar.

It had seemed like such a good idea at the time. I pictured a happy hour of parent/child bonding. We would amble with cautious speed through the leafy lanes of Sussex, me gently encouraging, coaching, and occasionally correcting Kelly's driving technique. I would speak in calm, measured tones, and she would be delighted to receive such expert instruction from her ever-loving father. It would be such a joyous, relaxing time. What transpired was as relaxing as the battle of Armageddon. Tension climbed as we gently brushed bushes and shrubs on the roadside, and edged even higher when we narrowly missed a warm embrace with an articulated truck. It wasn't Kelly's fault – she was a new driver. But her braking was, shall we say, sudden. A couple of times I found myself kissing the windscreen, my nose corrugated up against the unyielding glass. My impatience rose to dangerous levels. I even screamed loudly in tongues in an octave so high that it sounded like an excerpt from the Vienna Boys Choir's *Glossolalia* album.

But the fever pitch of agony came when we encountered a roundabout. Kelly was nervous (understandably, Saddam Hussein was teaching her to drive) and so stalled the car a couple of times. A driver waiting behind got impatient and honked his horn two or three times. I was ready to kill him. Eager to share a gesticulation not dissimilar to a 'one way' sign, I was utterly incensed at his crass lack of understanding. And then it occurred to me: I was angry with him for doing exactly what I had been guilty of for the last twenty minutes. He was mildly irritated with someone he didn't know; I was bursting a blood vessel over the driving of my daughter whom I dearly love. Why is it that we so often are the most intolerant with the sins of others that we ourselves are guilty of? It seems that a mad blindness seizes us, throwing into magnified, floodlit detail the small transgressions of those around us while we totally ignore – or are even oblivious to – the jumbo jet-sized failings in us. We strain at the gnat, and swallow a three-humped camel in the process.

Perhaps there is actually some mischief in our critical attitudes. We zero in on the specks of sins in others' lives, hoping that in so doing we will cover our own far darker stains. Deeply unhappy with our own grubbiness, we distil our shame and turn it into venom, ready for a snakebite that can fracture and destroy fellowship and friendship in seconds. So be careful that you don't beat others up just because you don't like what you see in the mirror. Remember that toxic words can kill.

And avoid the subtle snare of Satan: just buy your kids proper driving lessons.

THE RIDE

I was beginning to feel that my happy little plan to take the family on a horse ride was a serious mistake. Earlier in the day, fancying myself as an evangelical John Wayne, the idea of saddling up and riding through the sun-drenched Oregon trees had been appealing. I'd even taken to calling my wife 'Pardner', and suggested that we 'Mosey on down for a ride', although I confess I do not know what it is to mosey.

Now, as I bobbed up and down aboard this sweating brown monster that possessed neither a handbrake nor a safety belt, I was having second, and third thoughts. How was one supposed to steer this thing? Did this animal have any intention of being directed anywhere anyway? I was tempted to abandon the reins, and just hold on tight to Dobbin's ears with a grip that would have turned his eyes bloodshot. I wanted the ride to be over, *now*.

I tried chatting with the horse, but it was useless. I even tried a couple of horsey gags: 'Say, horse, why the long face?' etc. He ignored me, and then broke wind at length and with great volume. Like most men who think that flatulence is the sport of kings, I was impressed. My friends looked over their shoulders back at me with accusing eyes, utterly appalled.

'What? It's the horse . . . '

Twenty minutes later, my worst fears were realized. I was fifth in a line of about thirty tons of puffing horseflesh, when a cry went up. 'Kelly has been thrown!'

I imagined the horror of my then ten-year-old little girl, hurled like a rag doll into the air, and landing with a disabling thud. I panicked, kicked Dobbin, who responded immediately, and cantered up to where my daughter was laying on the ground, our friends already down at her side. She was screaming in pain, and her face was a mask of blood. I quite literally fell off my horse and ran to her side.

Every parent knows that fear travels through the brain at lightning speed. I thought that her neck was broken, and a speeded up film ran wildly before my eyes: scenes of wheelchairs, hospitals and surgeries. I was beside myself with panic. Dr Chris, our friend, was already checking her prone body for serious damage. Thank God, he was there. We were miles from the nearest hospital.

Richard, our son, was kneeling beside his sister, and he was crying too. Why was he in tears, I wondered?

'I just love her, I just love her . . . ' he sobbed out.

I was momentarily distracted. This uncharacteristic display of brotherly/sisterly affection was a miracle something akin to the raising of Lazarus.

My mind snapped back into focus as Kelly cried out again. Her back was in one piece, but she had broken an arm and separated her chin from her jawbone. Her face was smeared now with tear soaked mud mingling with bright red blood.

Something snapped inside me. I know that I should have been the mature father, someone to bring a sense of calm spiritual order into the chaos that we were feeling at that moment. Perhaps I should have gathered the family to pray, or just whispered words of comfort and care. But I didn't.

Instead, I chose to vent my pent up panic by throwing my head back and yelling a swear word at the top of my voice. I'm not proud of my stupid reaction, but it's the truth. And what happened next came as a complete surprise. Kelly stopped her screaming with pain, and turned her attention to her swearing Christian father.

'Dad! I can't believe you just said that word. How dare you . . . and you a Christian leader! You should be ashamed of yourself!' And with that, her high velocity rebuke delivered to a now sheepish parent, she turned her attention back to some more full-blooded screaming.

A few hours later, after Kelly had sat bravely in the local casualty ward while they picked debris out of her lower lip, we laughed at the moment when she had given me a good telling off. But I learned a lesson that day. It dawned on me that for impressionable Kelly, a father acting in a manner contrary to his publicly stated beliefs (I think the short description is 'hypocrite') was more painful than a broken arm and a mashed chin. Parents – and leaders – are called to be an example; children – and God's people – are like wet cement. We who lead are blessed with the privilege and responsibility of this mysterious thing called *influence*. We have the power to bless or stain the lives of those around us.

When Paul prodded Timothy with the pointed exhortation to 'be an example', he was reminding the young warrior that leadership is more than gifted oratory, or theological dexterity. It is not just about acquiring managerial skills or having the ability to motivate people to action. We are called to be examples – the Greek word is 'tupos' – which means to inscribe a wax tablet. Other lives are profoundly affected by our wise calligraphy or selfish scrawl.

But example is not to be confused with projecting the right image. I often meet Christian leaders who are anxious about being truly human. Frightened of 'letting the side down', they step back from any reference to their own fears, doubts and sins, and instead present a facsimile of virtue, which, ultimately, their very human followers fail to identify with.

Our example is not in the suggestion that we are without fault, but rather, in our determination to push ahead to follow Jesus, even though we struggle with the same things that beset those that we lead. Our commitment to holiness is expressed, not in the notion that we enjoy a false immunity to sin and temptation, but in the grace-kissed choices that we actually make each day as we choose the right pathway.

Hypocrisy is hurtful. Pretending helps no one. And I never want to be on Dobbin's back again . . . or indeed, standing behind him.

48 HOURS

I only knew Jane for 48 hours.

She was a beaming face in the crowd at a retreat that I was addressing in Texas, the picture of an enthusiastic Christian, which she was not. Her laughing eyes were not the result of faith: she was just glad to be around positive, happy people. Jane's seventeen-year-old life had been a catalogue of disappointment and rejection; her home smashed suddenly by divorce; her hopes dashed by the cold reality that neither parent really wanted her. She had been shunted around from one distant relative to another, like a pinball flipped carelessly away. Somehow, she had held on to the ability to smile. The Christian retreat in the blistering Texas hills was a shimmering, sweaty endurance test for us; for her, it was a cool oasis, where she could soak up the atmosphere of laughter and love, just for a while.

Three things happened to Jane in those 48 hours. The first could have snuffed out any possibility of her finding faith forever. The campground was being shared by another group of rather rabid, monochrome Christians who apparently knew just a bit more than God and were eager to let everyone else know it. They spotted her black *Metallica* T-shirt and pounced like evangelistic thugs.

'Do you listen to rock music?' they demanded, without troubling to introduce themselves. Jane did, and was happy to advertise the fact. Whereupon Jane was

advised that God would surely send her straight to a
burning hell if she did not revise her taste in music. The
God of the Universe was apparently a dedicated music
critic and huge consignments of human beings would be
cremated if their choice of CDs differed from his own.
Jane told them to mind their own business. They
stomped off, no doubt to pray for her wretched soul, and
to listen to a few Des O'Connor tracks.

The second thing that happened to Jane was that she
became a Christian. It was during the Saturday evening
meeting. The worship was warm, without being intense,
and Jane, without invitation, walked to the front, took
the microphone in her trembling hands, and told everyone that she was a thirty-second-old believer. With a rare
eloquence, she thanked the group for being so kind to
her, for being part of the reason that she had decided to
follow Christ. A welcome party broke out. People
clapped and cheered and lined up to hug Jane.

The third thing that happened to Jane was that she
bumped into the patrolling zealots again. Roving the
area in pursuit of anyone who might look flippantly
happy, they quizzed her this time about how much television she watched (relaxation is wasteful), what friends
she had (the unsaved are dangerous scum), but never
enquired as to whether she was even a Christian. Kay
and I found her sitting under a tree, her eyes bloodshot,
her crestfallen face wet with tears.

'I hate this stuff! This is why I didn't become a
Christian earlier! What right do they have to talk to me
like that? Who are they to tell me if I can watch TV or
not?'

We talked with Jane for about half an hour, and tried
to gently explain that following Jesus was costly, but one
was not required to follow the rules of bullying bigots.
We let her know that God was not firing up a barbecue

just for her, ready to toss her hell-bound, even when she made mistakes or strayed into sin. We just encouraged her, and prayed with her for a few moments too. We did nothing costly, sacrificial, or heroic. It was just a chat.

It was time to leave, and our car was waiting. We hugged Jane goodbye, and she seemed reluctant to let us go. Her parting words live with me now, over a year later. Her farewell both haunts and inspires me, unlikely as it is that we will ever see her again, this side of forever. Her eyes bright, and her tears gone, she smiled a massive grin.

'Goodbye Mum. Goodbye Dad.'

Sometimes, it doesn't take much.

WORSHIP

ARE WE DAFT?

It's an uncomfortable thought, and it sounds quite uncharitable to ask it, but I've had a persistent question nagging away at me recently: Are Christians actually quite stupid? Would a 'revival' mean the mass production of yet more somewhat daft people?

This potentially unkind question nipped at my ankles while I was watching a chap on Christian television recently. He was loudly offering the promise of guaranteed riches and hyper health, in exchange for a donation, to him of course. The fact that he himself looked about three hundred years old, on the brink of immediate death, and had the onscreen presence of a grinning ghost train skeleton seemed like a slight contradiction to my simple brain. He was proclaiming his message of massive riches from a building that looked like the inside of the gents at Waterloo Station, but that didn't deter what P.T. Barnum referred to as 'suckers' from calling in droves to take advantage of the offer. I was stunned. Why this rush of lemming-like believers willing to hurl themselves over the precipice of mindlessness? My wife has now banned me from watching the chap at breakfast or indeed any other time, as she doesn't like soggy Cornflakes down the television set.

I have been to an event where the speaker continuously emphasized two key messages. First, he regaled us with testimony about how his personal sense of security no longer comes from his ministry; no, the size of his

ministry is not important. Secondly, he peppered just
about every other sentence of his sermons with phrases
that told us all, loud and clear, just how his ministry is
big, growing, expanding, touching the nations, and is
generally intergalactic. People bought his tapes in
droves, oblivious to the glaring fact that, not only was he
not practising what he was preaching – he was not even
preaching what he had just been preaching, if you get
my drift. Mad.

I have witnessed further corporate stupidity in services when an apparent 'word of knowledge' is shared.
The landscape is perhaps familiar.

Leader: 'Mmmmm, thank you Lord, yes. Yes, there's
someone here tonight with a bad back. . . . '

(The crowd visibly cheers up, apparently oblivious to
the fact that probably at least 50 per cent of the people
present have got bad backs, due in part to the cheap metal
and canvas chairs purchased for a knockdown price from
the Brethren church that closed down last year.)

Leader: Yes, I can further say that this person with the
aforementioned back problem is either male . . .

. . . or female.

(Crowd looks around to scrutinize people of either
gender in the midst.)

Leader: 'Mmmm, there's more. This person with a
back tormented by Satan who is either male or female
was *born of a woman* . . . '

(Crowd amazingly impressed by this revelation, mut-
ters gasps of astonishment at this precision and accuracy.)

. . . And then there's that kind of 'praying for the sick'
when it's not just that people are being given a little
shove in order to help them fall over, which is bad
enough. But I've been in meetings where the evangelist
was using more karate chops that Jackie Chan.

I know that God describes us humans as being like sheep, which, let's face it, aren't that bright. But is it really that many of Jesus' followers have in fact permanently kissed their brains goodbye and are now dabbing mint sauce behind their ears? Was Josh McDowell right in his assertion that most Christians have only got two brain cells – one's gone missing and the other's gone looking for it?

Perhaps not. I just think that all too often we are so desperate for something, anything to happen, that we rush like Sahara-bound hikers to sip from any pool, no matter how muddy. But God's name isn't honoured by sleight of hand miracles; testimonies smattered with exaggeration; and Pavlovian congregations who are ready to jump whenever the leaders ring a bell.

We feel that we must buy in to belong, and that to think that something was meaningless perhaps betrays our own lack of depth and spirituality. I saw this in action when I attended a conference where the speaker shared what many described as 'deep' teaching. 'That was really deep' often actually means, 'I haven't got the first clue what he was rattling on about, how about you?' Everyone that I asked said that they thought the sermon was great. When I asked the follow-up question – what was it about – everyone looked clueless.

And there's another internal conspiracy that, in the desperate desire to believe, and to be positive, we feel that we might be letting the side down if we ask awkward questions. But a genuinely enquiring mind is actually a sign of faithfulness, not treachery. Questioning shows a hunger for the authentic rather than the superficially satisfying that fails any close inspection. Cynicism is deathly, but opening our mouths and swallowing everything wholesale ultimately brings discredit to the good name of God.

So think, for God's sake.

VERY HUMAN WORSHIP . . .

Years ago, I led a church where we practised 'open worship' every Sunday morning. This meant that there was a rather scary and occasionally wonderful part of the service, normally for around thirty minutes, when anyone in the congregation could pray, read scripture, prophesy, or – somewhat more worryingly – begin to lead the whole church in the spontaneous singing of a worship song. The latter was always a bit frightening, and was often quite excruciating. Someone would 'feel led' to strike up a song which had originally been composed in the key of C; but now it had been pitched it wrongly in the key of F sharp. So it was, in the higher bits, that 150 people were to be heard frantically shrieking in falsetto. The keyboard player would be desperately stabbing every part of the piano to try to locate the elusive key. I really should have stepped up to re-pitch the song, but cowardice reigned: the mournful screaming continued.

'Prayer request time' could be a bit awkward too – anyone could stand and ask for prayer for, well, anything. One morning a lady requested prayer for her teenage son, who, to quote her exactly, 'had twisted his testicles'. Many were unsure as to whether this condition was figurative or literal. The boy concerned, being present, looked as if he would never appear in public again; his beetroot face was quite fluorescent. But there was much intercession in response to this most painful need: some raised their hands in prayer – and a few of the brothers were obviously labouring in vicarious identification with the chap with the unfortunate testicular chaos. They crossed their legs and wept at the thought of it.

And of course there were the inevitable daft prophecies, which ranged from the harmlessly innocuous reminder that our Lord was coming soon, so 'hold tight and he'd talk to us later', to the more bizarre pronouncements: 'Do not fear, my people; these are scary times. Once in a while, I, the Lord your God, get a bit scared myself . . . '

We were very, very spiritual, but there were occasional moments when glorious humanity crept in, and one could imagine a wry smile breaking out in heaven.

One delightful elderly gentleman obviously found the whole thing exhausting, and would often snooze during the prayers. This was fine until his tonsils and nose decided to contribute to the occasion with ear-shattering snoring. Some felt led to pray for the jumbo jet that was apparently flying overhead, while others wondered just who was wielding a chainsaw in the service, or perhaps riding a throaty Harley Davidson around the place. The snoring was getting louder.

When it was time for the sermon, I coughed loudly in a crude attempt to bring him back to consciousness. Still he snored. As my talk was on spiritual warfare, I thought that perhaps I could stir the congregation in general – and the blissful sleeper in particular, with a loud, cheerleading exclamation.

'The devil is defeated!' I roared with gusto.

It worked. He woke up, and responded to my rallying call without hesitation: 'Bless his lovely name!' he shouted back, his eyelids still heavy with sleep.

There was an immediate flurry of concern – had our dear brother converted to Satanism? Not a bit. He just got woken up at the wrong time.

All of which reminds me that we should never lose sight of our humanity when we come to worship. Worshipping God should be taken absolutely seriously – but we shouldn't take ourselves too seriously in the process. When all is said and done, however contained and ordered and thoughtful our worship, or however contemporary and musically brilliant we might be, we're still ultimately a bunch of idiots desperately doing our best to focus on the sublime. We falter in our praying, subject angels to unimaginable suffering with our singing, and our attempts to fathom out what God might be saying through the prophetic are sometimes laughable. Our sermons, which seek to plumb the depths of the divine are often loaded with stuttering, clichéd platitudes. And it's not that we're intentionally ungodly, or false prophets worthy of stoning. We're just human. And God knows it.

ALTAR CALLS

It was the moment that I both loved and dreaded. The sermon had ended, the speaker's Bible had been closed – and now, it was time for the congregation to do their bit. Invariably, I used to be one of the first people to respond.

This part of the service is called by a variety of names, according to your tribe and tradition: some dub it the 'altar call', others the 'response', or 'ministry time'. And of course, some churches don't have them at all – while others don't consider that they've had a kosher Christian meeting without a pause for open response at the end of almost every service. In some churches, gentle background music is provided, while others stoically respond in stern silence. Sometimes the respondent is just required to raise a hand, or stand for prayer – and there are of course the Billy Graham-style come-down-to-the-front-*now* shuffling moments too. Salvationists have their 'penitents benches' – and I've visited Pentecostal churches in the USA that have wooden 'altars' with built in tissue dispensers conveniently provided for the tearful.

Like anything else in church life, these so-called altar calls can be abused and manipulated, or become yet another empty ritual that is more about affirming that the speaker has said something useful than anything more deeply significant. (*Result! Loads of people came forward!*) And some altar calls insult one's intelligence, particularly when the speaker begins by asking for volunteers for martyrdom, but, seeing few takers, ends up by giving the impression that you should be at the front, *right now*, if you've ever eaten breakfast at some time in your life. I also fear the 'Nescafe' spirituality that can result from being told that, whatever the issue, it would be sorted, instantly, if you'll only take a quick stroll in the direction of the pulpit.

But for the most part, these can be positive times. We are in the church, which is a community where we constantly make choices to align our lives with Jesus – and where some prayerful support of those around us is helpful.

In my Christian youth, I responded to these appeals at every opportunity. I was rabidly desperate to please God, and I would rush forward to respond at the end of any and every sermon, regardless of the content. I was surely every preacher's dream, ever ready as I was to make a quick dash in yet another flush of recommitment. Sometimes my response bore no relationship to any kind of reality. If the preacher had asked for any Taiwanese dyslexic basket weavers in the house to go forward for prayer, I would have been found at the front, ready for a career in wicker. A call for volunteers for a leader of the local 'Women Aglow' chapter would have found me eagerly front bound offering my piloting skills to those flaming sisters.

But one consistent factor stands out from my spiritual sprinting down a hundred naves and aisles – almost invariably, I went forward to *apologise*. Like a whipped puppy flinching because of the expectation of yet another slap, I assumed that God would only ever have words of critique and complaint to shout at arch-sinner Lucas. The possibility that he might want to encourage, strengthen, or simply let me know that I was doing okay never occurred to me. Ever.

And so I repented of a few things that weren't actually sin. One sunny evening I went forward to apologise to God for feeling happy, as if a feeling of anything less than pure *joy* was unworthy. I also went forward to repent of my feelings towards Kay – now my wife. Surely, I reasoned, it could not possibly be God's will that I marry her – after all, I fancied . . . er, I mean I found her attractive. Having been schooled in the view that God's beautiful plan for my life would probably be precisely the opposite of anything that I might like, I deduced that I'd have to marry someone really ugly.

I've just finished a lengthy study of the Seven Churches of Revelation, and was stunned to discover that to two of them, Jesus had *no* word of rebuke at all – only commendation and a verbal pat on the back. The lack of rebuke is . . . shocking. Why are we more at home with the threat of judgement, but struggle with the idea that God might want to tell us that we're doing all right?

Perhaps there's a big surprise waiting for us when we finally step forward on the last day, when we see Jesus face to face. Is it possible that it won't be heaven itself that leaves us breathless – it won't be the megaton singing of exuberant angelic choirs that blows us away on that day, or the first sightseeing of a new city where the Lamb will be our light? Perhaps the hugest shock of all will be the sight of a perfect God, whispering the most unexpected greeting to plebs like us: 'Well done, good and faithful servant.'

WELCOME HOME

The plane was jam-packed; every seat taken; every over-head crammed with stuff. The transatlantic trip had been especially bad, as the chap next to me had decided to grope the female passenger seated next to him – with whom he had not been previously acquainted – while she was asleep. Statements were taken, and the police were waiting to meet the plane and cart him off.

Finally, the eternal flight ended, and I came up the escalator into the arrivals area. It was loaded with eager, waving people who were there to welcome folks home. People clutching cards with names hastily scrawled on them were scanning the arriving masses, their smiling eyes alive with expectation. Children holding balloons looked out excitedly for Daddy. Men holding flowers craned their necks to search for the familiar face of a homecoming daughter. And for one mad, irrational moment, I stood there and searched hopefully for a card that bore *my* name. Of course, it was ridiculous, illogical even. My car was parked at the airport, and there was not a single reason why anyone should form a welcom-ing party for me. But after eighteen hours of anonymity, I felt the urgent need of some simple warmth and friendly recognition. Obviously, I searched for a balloon or a name card in vain.

I did, however, get a balloon – or the emotional equiv-alent thereof – during a visit to Jerusalem a couple of weeks ago. The group that I was part of were wandering through the Hassidic area of the city – a ghetto, really – the exclusive domain of the ultra-conservative Jewish traditionalists. At the edge of the orthodox area, a huge notice warns that modest clothing must be worn at all times. The darkened streets teem with men with those hair ringlets that dangle, with big black trilby hats in plentiful supply. Some wore long silver gowns with bearskin headwear. We, in our western dress, looked completely out of place, like day-trippers from another planet.

Finally, we arrived at one of the meeting halls. We were uninvited tourists really, on a spot-the-Pharisee safari. Our team leader disappeared inside. A few moments later, we nervously climbed the stairs to look for him.

Inside the hall were around two hundred men and boys, all of them dressed in the antiquated style of their tradition. They sat around tables, chattering, eating and drinking. Some rocked back and forth in the rhythm of prayer; others talked urgently, voracious students, copies of the Torah open before them. We just stood in the entrance area, watched and waited. Suddenly, one of the men came towards us, his face wreathed in a huge grin of greeting. Without asking who we were or where we were from, he ushered us into the hall, waving aside our reluctance to intrude with a repeated 'come, come, come'. They sat us down at a table, bought us snacks and drinks, and tried to engage in conversation, which was difficult as they spoke *Yiddish*.

Then the singing began, a strange, plaintive cry, a spontaneous song without words. There was no worship leader. One of the men would strike up the lilting refrain, which then echoed down the tables as the men sobbed out their song. I have never been a fan of all those Jewish worship songs, mainly because they all end with everyone shouting 'Oy' and I always yell the 'Oy' just after everyone else, which is embarrassing. In fact, I've never been that keen on those Hebraic moments in worship conferences when some enthusiastic chap decides to sound a long blast on the obligatory rams horn, the *shophar*. Everyone else usually gets very excited at that bit, and there is much yelling of 'Hallelujah' and head-butting of beribboned tambourines, but I'm not really into it. The obscene squawk that is produced actually sounds like someone filling a cow's bottom with compressed air. Not that inspiring, to me at least. But there was something enchanting about this song. We listened, hushed and respectful.

And then they stood to their feet, and began to move around the room, hands on each other's shoulders, in a kind of walking dance, the sad song now turning to an ode to joy. And suddenly, they were at our table, beckoning us to join their circle. It was impossible to resist. In fact, we all wanted to be a part of this bizarre routine. Round and round we went, singing our hearts out as we did.

Thirty minutes later, we had bid our farewells, and we were back out on the streets once more. But the welcome that they had given us was unforgettable. We had not joined their community, or embraced their ethics or traditions. But they had allowed us into the heart of what they were doing, and we had walked with them for a brief, blessed while. I learned something about church that day. The church is a community that embraces ethics and disciplines. Those who would follow Christ and therefore be part of it, enter a voluntary arena where there are, rightly, expectations about the kind of lives that we are to live. But we must also be a people who allow rampant 'sinners' to travel with us, eat with us, and dance with us. The grimy and the rampantly immoral should still catch a glimpse of a blue balloon or a card with their name on when they bump into us.

Such a welcome will make an indelible impression. That's why, try as I may, I can't get that lilting Hassidic song out of my head.

LEFT BEHIND

The meeting was going quite well, or so I thought. The building was filled with ardent worshippers downstairs, but an empty balcony yawned above us. I closed my eyes again and continued to worship. Kay tugged my arm insistently, her voice a whispered, but urgent hiss.

'Quick! Look up into the balcony.'

I peered once again up into the cavernous space, and affirmed that it was indeed a nice piece of architecture, surely one of the more attractive balconies that I'd seen in a while. Kay gave me one of those 'When did you do a brain exchange with a donkey?' looks. I was puzzled. Confused. I said so. 'I'm puzzled and confused.'

Another when-did-you-last-chew-on-a-carrot look. 'Look up there, can you see them?'

Now I was interested. The balcony was empty. Them?

'The demons. Two of them. They're taking a bodily form and they're leaning over the balcony, laughing at us. Do you see them now?'

At this point, I need to point out two important facts. The first is that my dear wife is very normal, balanced and sane. She doesn't see forty thousand visions a day, she is highly rational and very calm and does not believe that anything that goes wrong in life is due to the notion that Beelzebub is camping in our bathroom. She would be the last one to engage in super-spiritual fantasies. And the second fact is, that, as hard as I tried, I couldn't see anything other than a vacant balcony. I felt highly carnal as I stood there, at first squinting (didn't help), and then closing my eyes and then opening them again quickly. Standing on one leg while speaking in tongues didn't cause me to see them either. There was nothing – at least, nothing that I could see.

Kay could still see them. 'What are we going to do?' she whispered urgently.

My response was quite brilliant, even though I say so myself. I wanted to say, *'We'll get you medication. We'll see a doctor. We'll lock you up. Pick any one of the above.'* But instead, I came out with a piece of supercilious twaddle that at least got me off the hook and prevented us from inviting the whole congregation to look up and stare at nothingness.

'Darling, we're here to worship Jesus. Demons love attention – so let's ignore them and get on with what matters, shall we?' I smiled, I wasn't sure that she was wholly convinced, but it would do for the moment. We finished the service without doing any collective balcony spotting.

Kay didn't mention what she'd seen to anyone, for which I was grateful, and I certainly didn't say a word. Why would I? The next morning, the minister of the church spent some time chatting with us and our team about the evening we'd enjoyed together, and asked if we would mind spending some time praying in their church building before we left town.

He had an odd request – or maybe not so odd. 'I'm not being weird or spooky or anything – but could you spend some concentrated time praying in the balcony?'

Kay shot me a look. I ignored it. 'Why – do you have some structural problems up there? Plaster cracking, eh? Replacement beams needed?'

The Minister hesitated. 'Well . . . actually, the problem is spiritual. There's such a dark atmosphere up there

– and we've sensed that there's a real demonic presence . . . '

Kay shot me another look. I ignored it.

'We've had problems up there for years. It seems that it all started when the choir in this church fell out with a previous minister – they developed such a hatred for him that they decided to go on strike during a Sunday morning service – they were trying to embarrass him into leaving. They met up in that balcony to hatch their plan. Since then – there's been this weird presence.'

We stomped around in that balcony and prayed and bound and loosed and did everything we could think of that didn't involved crucifixes and garlic. And I learned that day that there is a serious power in agreement and collusion – both negatively and positively. Twenty-five years earlier, a group came together in an anarchic covenant, and the dark legacy of their determined contract – forged in the balcony – remained for decades. Groups can be invaded – the theological term is structural sin – as evil resides in corporations, governments and even denominations and church boards. But what is true negatively, is also true dynamically for the kingdom of God. Jesus called us into a praying agreement together, making it clear that there is a greater authority in the collective than in the personal.

Feel free to dismiss the demons in the balcony as bats in the belfry or odd charismatic imagination if you will, but know that, all of our relationships leave a legacy, they are the cause of an effect. The result is often visible – and sometimes, I venture – invisible. Whatever your view on these things, allow yourself to be challenged with this thought, as I am: what do I leave behind?

JESUS

MIND THE GAP

Yesterday, I was served a hamburger by a deer.

The management of my local fast food eatery had required their smiling staff to wear large, scarlet antlers festooned with blinking fairy lights. For background music, a track from the compilation CD *Now That's What I Call Music To Go Mad By* warbled

Christmas is a time for us to be together
Christmas is a time for us to love each other . . .

I glanced around the restaurant. A lady and her husband sat silently at a corner table. There was something vaguely menacing about the way she tore tiny, carnivorous bites out of her burger. Occasional frosty glares were exchanged; palpable tension crackled between them like static electricity. And over in the other corner, another chirpy family outing unravelled as a manic infant swirled milkshake around his head, gloriously baptizing nearby tut-tutting tables in strawberry.

Suddenly the gap between the *image* of Christmas – as it's supposed to be – and the *reality* of how it actually is yawned before me like the Grand Canyon. Is that gap part of the reason why some find the whole business of Christmas depressing? Marital tensions, life draining diseases and worries about redundancy are pressures that don't take time off for Christmas, politely disappearing for the cheery season and popping back in after

Boxing Day. The idea of a happy-zone magical season can taunt us with its sheer unreality, especially if one is required to share the festivities with distant family members who irritate you into assassination fantasies before the Queen has even begun her afternoon national chat.

The unreality has spread to the reason for the season itself. I have a few Christmas cards where artists have daubed the traditional Nativity scene in unreal colours, tarting it all up with a false, garish glory. A surreally calm Mary, who apparently chose to give birth while dressed from head to foot as a blue nun, glows with soft fluorescence, courtesy of a goldfish bowl-shaped halo. Joseph is usually absent from the scene. Perhaps he's out the back trying to straighten out a wonky coffee table he made earlier. And baby Jesus, himself adorned with a junior-sized goldfish bowl, is sitting up already, and appears to be thanking the wise men for coming to his party. All rather good for one who is but thirty-minutes old. Grinning cattle peer at the family from neat hay bales that whiff of Chanel N°5. Lovely.

Even the old Carol suggests a scene of blatant unreality

> The cattle are lowing, the baby awakes
> But little Lord Jesus no crying he makes.

Oh really? Why wouldn't Jesus cry then? Perhaps he'd alert all and sundry to the fact that he needed his swaddling clothes changing with a raised hand of blessing rather than a heartfelt scream, him being the Son of God and all.

Much trouble was caused when a speaker suggested that Jesus went to the toilet while upon this earth – as if we didn't know. But there was a furore among some, who insisted that this was a blasphemy. But what on

earth do they think he did for thirty-three years? It's just
the loo is just so . . . ordinary, so functional, so human.

The irony is that Christmas is about the story of the
extraordinary God kissing a very ordinary world. The
true splendour of the Nativity is the notion of a God
landing without much fanfare or fuss, welcomed by a
few night workers and travelling mystics. The King
shows up in squalor. Like a heavenly bungee jumper, he
shunned the pristine order of heaven to dive down into
our sweaty, confused, fogbound world, and announced
a new order of living. Christmas says that we no longer
need to haul ourselves heavenward by our own boot-
laces, but that God comes to rescue those who whisper
an invitation.

Christmas: it's about the God who is willing to close
the gap.

PARTY MIRACLES

'The whorehouse', the locals used to call it. The large, imposing church building had become an object of scorn in the town. Two previous ministers had seduced members of their flock, and word of it had spread throughout the community. Scandal lives long: for years the members of that church hung their heads in shame, clinging together, but turning inward. Reacting to the promiscuity of the past, they descended into another, more respectable immorality – legalism. Theirs was a negative Christianity, defined by what they *didn't* do. Stifling rules regulated their behaviour. Fun was starched out of them. Their faith was as rigid as ice, and just as cold. They thought that those who drank wine would one day be sent to hell by the Jesus who launched his ministry at Cana. Dancing, bowling, television, and anything fun were outlawed. They were fanatically zealous in their Pentecostal prohibitions.

And then, ever so slowly, a springtime thaw began. A little nervously at first, they began to laugh more during their gatherings. Worship became more up-tempo, and they discovered that clapping hands and dancing feet are close cousins. The lifeblood that is new Christians began to appear; legalism was sent packing, and exchanged for a hearty, hopeful faith. The locals forgot that the whorehouse had ever been so called.

It all came to a head last week. The weekly prayer and Bible study meeting had been cancelled in favour of a

Valentines Supper. A witty sermonette was delivered.
They played some silly games. And then a band took the
stage – which included two deacons in its line-up.
People sat respectfully around tables as the musicians
moved into some catchy dance numbers. Fingers were
tapped on tables; feet moved in time beneath the white
cloths. And then suddenly, James stood up. He is a giant
of a man who could break your back with his hug. Three
years ago, he was in prison, and might have felt inclined
to do so, but he had since got to know Jesus. He asked
his minister if it was okay – and then invited his wife to
dance. Arm in arm, the two swept around what had
become a dance floor, while the rest of the church
applauded and laughed at the sheer unbridled joy of it
all. Ian, another deacon, asked his wife to dance, and she
complied gladly. And then John, an elderly man who
had lived too many angry years in the shroud of scowl-
ing religiosity, and had never danced in his forty years of
married life, asked his wife if she would do him the honour. She couldn't, because she didn't know how – but
was thrilled by his invitation.

Soon the floor was jammed with people, a celebration
of fun and fidelity. And among them, a couple who had
been separated for a while, and for whom divorce had
looked very likely; in each other's arms now, a new
beginning, a miracle at a party, a surprise indeed.

But then again, Jesus enjoys party miracles. He
seemed more at home with the full-blooded laughter of
long meals with friends and the so-called silly giggling
of fidgety children than with the austere, cardboard
'goodness' of the religious crowd. He seemed to find
their moratorium on fun as restrictive as a fishbone
corset, try as they did to pull it tight around him. Party
poopers can sneer in derision, and the sworn, stiff ene-
mies of so-called frivolity can wait outside in the cold of

their making, but as the band played and the people danced that Valentine's night away, there was a light in their eyes, a borrowed, reflected light from him.

PURPOSE, POWER AND POSTCODES

I do get lost rather a lot. My oft-repeated geographical bewilderment is entirely my own fault, although I do sometimes try to blame Kay, my longsuffering map-clutching wife. Yes, there are seasons of navigational tension in our marriage.

My getting lost is usually due to one reason – I don't like listening to directions. I can read a map and even a road sign, but I do get bored rather easily, which is not helpful when someone is performing one of those extended 'third traffic light and then turn left and straight on at the next roundabout' types of monologue. I begin with good intentions. Having got lost, I stop at the kerbside by someone who is either (a) wearing a compass pinned to their anorak or (b) looks like they might have succeeded at geography in school. I then wind down the window and ask the way: this should surely be easy enough. But then I become aware that I am no longer listening to this helpful pedestrian, who is kindly trying to help me to get my life back on track. I switch off and wander into a mental blur halfway through their giving the instructions. 'Turn left, second right at the Dog and Duck . . . ' and now my eyes are glazed over, my eyelids drooping. My erstwhile would-be guide, sensing that perhaps I did not listen as attentively as I should have the first time (my snoring is a hint), proceeds to tell me the way, *slooooowly*, *methodically* . . . all over again – and by

173

this time, my chin is on my chest and I'm a gonner for the night. Cosmetic surgery would be good, but not for a facelift: I wish I could have one of those satellite navigational devices implanted in my left armpit. Not knowing where on earth I am just seems to come naturally to me.

I've even got lost – *indoors*. As guest speaker at a church in Canada last weekend, I visited the gentleman's room before the service. Getting in there was easy, but when it came to getting out of the place, I was stymied. For five minutes I wrestled with the door handle, pushing, pulling, wondering if my whitened skeleton would be found in the gents twenty years from now, martyred by being locked in the church toilet. Then I noticed that there was *another* door on the opposite wall. I had turned around in the loo, and had been trying to find my way out through the (locked) sanitary supplies cupboard. People sometimes ask me big questions, such as 'Where is the church going?' and 'What is God doing in the UK right now?' How should I know? I can't even get out of the gents.

But just this week I reached a new pinnacle of stupidity in this lostness; it was a veritable Everest of inane behaviour. Deciding to book a hotel online, I made my reservation, and then came up with the brilliant idea of also getting precise on-line driving instructions that would effortlessly guide me from where we were to the hotel's exact location. All I needed was to put the postcode of the hotel into the Internet programme, press *enter* and, in an instant, my list of directions appeared. Easy! I felt rather smug as I printed the instructions off – this would beat squinting at a map in the half-light of the evening; no mounting frustration and 'shall we turn the car round here?' What a marvellous and labour-saving thing technology is, I mused . . .

Three hours later, I wanted to take my IBM Pentium Beelzebub 666 Laptop and just lob it out of the car. Two things happened, neither of which were the fault of the computer, but then why confuse the issue with that kind of logic? First, the on-line driving instructions had apparently been compiled by a witch coven that had made a sworn vow to get Christian leaders hopelessly adrift. The oh-so-confident directions told me to get off the safe but slow M25 to disappear into a jet-black labyrinth of Essex lanes, many of which had seen neither man nor beast in years. Up and down and round and round the moonless maze we drove, praying for a pub or petrol station – anything. (Strange thing to pray really, isn't it? As if God is supposed to build one on the spot somewhere just in response to our frantic request.) When we finally drove down a lane that came to an abrupt halt, because someone had recently built a house across it, turning it into a cul-de-sac, I knew that something was very, very wrong.

An hour and a half later – a period that was not at any point peppered with the sound of worship songs being duetted in our motor – we were back on the familiar M25, heading in the general area of the hotel, only to discover that when I had copied the postcode of the hotel into the driving instructions, that was the *only* information that I had noted about our accommodation for the night.

'Where are we staying then?' Kay asked innocently.

'IL5 2QY', I replied nonchalantly, as if hotels everywhere were so named.

I won't bore you with the details of how we finally checked into our postcode, but suffice it to say that what ought to have been a one-hour journey turned into a three-hour marathon of frustration – and, again, it was all down to me. See? I'm brilliant. Far from having all the answers for life's intricate navigation, I stumble around from one epic blunder to another like a born-again

Mr Bean. And in this case, the reason is simple – so breathless was I, so desperate to jump into the journey, that I did not take the twenty seconds needed to note the name and address of the hotel.

My experience did give me insight into a malady that characterises more of my life than I'd like to admit. In a sense, my postcode dilemma was not a one-off. Metaphorically, I really do spend much of my life hurtling around at speed, doing the 'Lord's work', but then wondering how much he is actually in or even vaguely near what I'm chasing after. I want my life to be precisely targeted, specially directed – but often I find myself in a blur, a frantic fog, hoping to hit the mark, but worried much of the time that I might be busily doing nothing. My face is fixed in concentration as I hurry breathlessly on, and my fingers are gripped knuckle white around the steering wheel – but all my intensity doesn't mean that I'm really walking in what he has initiated.

I end up sprinting around like a turbo-sheep, like mutton on adrenaline, dashing about in the general direction of the will of God, but ending up settling for survival rather than being truly alive. We know that Jesus said that without him we can do nothing – it's just that often we just don't believe him, and even if we do, we like to give it our best shot on our own anyway.

It's not that we're not busy, with all our efforts, meetings and services. But if God is not the initiator and director of our lives, they will ultimately not amount to much. The fruit of our busyness will be meagre; and we will feel like we're lost in the lanes of our own making. That's why I have come to believe that we should all ask ourselves a question daily: 'What is my purpose?'

What are the banner headlines that God has written over my life – and yours? Every one of us, whether we are in so-called 'full time' ministry or not, have been born for the purposes of God. I believe that there are things that we alone can uniquely achieve. Perhaps that's why we need to take our foot off the accelerator and take time out for reflection and reorientation, taking regular rest stops in our daily journeys. In the Psalms, there is a little word that we could so easily skip over or miss altogether: 'Selah'. I'm told that it means, 'stop and think about it'.

I'm one of those people who don't like to stop off at the petrol station to refuel. I tend to set a completely unnecessary stopwatch at the beginning of a journey and then drive as fast as is legal in order to beat my own world records. Filling up is a second-sapping distraction, and thus I peer fearfully at the petrol gauge for much of the trip, terrified as the needle falls slowly to the 'E'. You can guess that, with this slightly manic disposition, I find it difficult to pull over at the 'Selah' services too.

But if my legacy is to be more than a set of worn tyres, I must ask God the real $64,000 question – 'Why am I here?'

There's another question that we should confront ourselves with, and that is, 'Where does my power come from?' My problem is that, having got the slightest hint of God's purposes for me, I then head off and then desperately try to fulfil them – in my own strength. Instead of genuinely seeking to walk in the energy and enabling of God, I become proficient, and then independent. Sadly, often when levels of expertise go up, correspondingly our levels of dependency go down. That's why good and great churches get into danger – after a while, they become so good at what they do, that they don't need God, and wouldn't miss him, at least for a while, if he vacated their area.

Jesus was a precision instrument when he was on earth; he never made waves, but surfed the waves that

his father made. Life for Jesus was an adventure into
what his father was doing, and joining in with it in the
power of the Holy Spirit. He was no entrepreneur, but
rather a delighted, submitted partner.

Surely that was the secret of his poise. Think about
the megaton weight of the world that he carried on his
shoulders. His was the most important agenda in the
history of agendas. He had the most important
message that has ever been to proclaim, a somewhat
slow-learning and dim-witted team to train, and
countless demands on his time from leaders who
wanted to draw him into interrogation and debate. He
was constantly pressed by sick people who urgently
needed healing, and hordes who were like lost sheep
without a shepherd. All this he carried, together with
the knowledge that he was marching daily ever closer,
not only to the most agonising death, but also to the
unthinkable weight of the work of redemption as well.
But in all of this, we never see him dashing around,
bowing to the demands of others, disorientated or
emotionally fractured by the pressure. Pressurised
beyond belief in Gethsemane, he turns to his father
and to his friends. But he is without panic, irritability,
moodiness, or any of the host of the responses that
seem to characterise pressurised us. One writer
famously observes:

'It is refreshing and salutary, to study the poise and
quietness of Christ. His task and responsibility might
well have driven a man out of his mind. But he was
never in a hurry, never impressed by numbers, never a
slave of the clock. He was acting, he said, as he observed
God to act – never in a hurry'.[1]

---

[1] J.B. Phillips

Perhaps the disciplines of reflection and contemplation need to get a makeover. The word 'meditation' has been hijacked and sparks a picture in our minds of some spiritual contortionist who sits with his legs crossed for hours; he is sniffing the wafty aroma of a joss stick; there is Enya music softly playing in the background. He crunches his eyes tight in order to go deeper – into himself.

And lest we Christians jump to a posture of superiority about these things, we have to face the fact that we haven't always done well with retreat and reflection, allowing these things to be hijacked by asceticism, legalism and downright extremes. So determined were they to run a mile – or fifty – from the big bad world, that they ended up rejecting some of the very wonderful gifts that God has lavished upon us for our enjoyment – like food, sleep, and sex. No one can deny their enthusiasm and commitment – but they were wrong, and a hangover still lingers over the idea of retreat, silence, and any kind of monastic experience as a result. Some medieval ascetics could boast that they had not lain down to sleep for fifty years.

Macarius of Alexandria ate no cooked food for seven years. Deliberately exposing his naked body to poisonous flies, he slept in a marsh for six months. Others kept a record of how many years it had been since they had even set eyes upon a woman.

The more famous Simeon Stylites (AD 309–459) built a column six feet high in the Syrian Desert. He became dissatisfied with its size and found one sixty feet high, and three feet across, where he sat for thirty years, exposed to the elements day after relentless day. He was drenched by rain, scorched by the sun, and chilled by the cold. Friends and disciples used a ladder to take him food and remove his waste. To prevent him from plummeting to

an untimely death while sleeping, he bound himself to
the pillar by a rope, which dug deep into his flesh, putre-
fied around it, stank, and teemed with worms. Simeon
picked up the worms which fell from his sores and
replaced them there saying to them, 'Eat what God has
given you.' Very nasty, except for the worms I suppose.

The Irish saint St Finnchua spent seven years suspended by his armpits in iron shackles. He and St Ite
deliberately allowed their bodies to be eaten by beetles.
St Ciaran mixed his bread with sand, and St Kevin
refused to sit down for seven years. Wearing hair shirts,
self-flagellation and involuntary dancing were all practised by the rival orders of St Francis and St Dominic.
Clarissa never washed after conversion, except her fin-
gertips; it was said that 'she dropped vermin while she
walked'.

So it is that charismatics like me, who like to turn the
volume up, and evangelicals generally, who are often
into projects, programmes and are more naturally
activists rather than contemplatives, need to rediscover
the power of silence. Ministers in mainline denominations have much to teach those, for example, in the new
churches, about the power of having a sabbatical, and of
having a spiritual director. We have reacted badly to the
past, and have become breathless workaholics as a
result. My friend Phil Wall is right when he points us
towards 'contemplative activism'.

So, for God's sake, and for yours, slow down. Take a
breath. Look around. Check your bearings, and check
the map. That dark Essex night, we finally checked into
our postcode hotel weary, frustrated, and just glad that
the trip was over. I don't want to feel the same when I get
to the last day of my life. So unashamedly, stop, pause,
take a breath – and, as Jesus did, enjoy the journey.

JESUS THE PREACHER

Pick an *exciting* word – any word will do.

Here are a few possibles that, for better or worse, might end up on a popular list of words associated with excitement:

'Ferrari' 'Skiing' 'Sex' 'Mountaineering' 'Lottery' 'Football'

And here's a word not likely to make the list:

'Sermon'

Hardly an exhilarating term, now is it? Most people might put the *sermon* word on their 'boring things to avoid like food poisoning' list. It speaks to many of an endless, monotone drone reserved for stuffy Sunday mornings. Bottom numbed by a bad chair and an eye superglued to the clock, whose minute hand doth not turn tangibly. An exercise in studied tedium hardly likely to quicken a pulse or a put a spring in your step. Something Christians listen to once each week to prove that they are really committed, a kind of evangelical hair shirt. But hardly exciting . . .

But when Jesus preached, it was riveting. No bland, colourless platitudes from him, just words that smacked home like a solid punch on the jaw. No twilight zone here's-a-little-thought-for-the-day from him, but the impact of a blinding searchlight shattering the blackness of a moonless night sky. They said he was like no one else, and not just because of style, or oratory, but also because of the weighty solid authority with which he

delivered his pithy preaches. And he was particularly
unlike the numbing religious crowd with their sophisti-
cated, irrelevant, I'm-better-than-the-rest-of-you-pagan-
filth mutterings.

I'd like to have got a ticket for the Sermon on the
Mount. I wonder how they advertised it. Were there
posters screaming, 'Today. Hillside. The Miracle Worker.
One day only. Free'? Of course, when someone's
trekking around the hillside opening blind eyes and
opening deaf ears, no commercials are usually required.
People just show up: clamouring hordes of them, desperately eager for a glimpse of a world that had been
beyond their own horizons.

When Jesus trudged up that hillside two thousand
years ago and sat down to deliver his talk, he calmly
lobbed a couple of dozen verbal grenades into the crowd
– and the reverberations and aftershocks are still being
felt to this day. Jesus, the King of the Hill, calmly told his
listeners how to really live. It was mind-blowing stuff,
radical and revolutionary enough to launch a crowd-
wide sharp intake of breath. In a presentation that would
have taken just over fourteen minutes to deliver, Jesus
demolished just about every popular idea about so-
called 'successful' living – false ideas that are still doing
the tired old rounds today – and presented a totally new
order of living. The crowd were amazed. These
oppressed people who had no land to call their own,
living as they did under the heel of the Roman occupy-
ing forces, heard about a King and a Kingdom that was
bigger than land, ethnicity, and the planet earth itself.
They heard about a different order of living, where self
and personal survival aren't king, but where Jesus takes
the throne. The Pharisees lingering on the borders of the
crowd would have been shocked to hear of a new order
of righteousness, which was not just about parading

your piety in public, but rather about caring for the last, the least, and the lost.

Stunned, the crowd gasped as they heard how everyone was welcomed by this new, Good King. How they could have a new quality of relationships. How sexual purity and marital fidelity was important and achievable under the reign of this Good Lord. How words can so easily hurt or help, and how the King invited all of them to offer every single area of their lives to his leadership. And most shocking and truly exciting of all was the news that this King was no distant monarch who locked himself behind luxurious closed palace doors. Rather, the King of Love himself had come to where they were and invited them all to enjoy a never-ending life of friendship with his royal self: the *real* people's King. And all of this came through Jesus the preacher.

Jesus' preaching was mind-stretching, challenging, encouraging, fun and life-changing. But one thing is certain – boring, it never was.

But because much of our preaching is just that – dull – there are some who react against it, pronouncing it as a clumsy, outmoded dinosaur, a tedious relic of yesteryear that has no place in the modern high-tech chat room that is our culture. And large events where the Bible is taught are particularly targeted. In a recent book, most of the contents of which I heartily endorse (indeed, I happily wrote the foreword), there is the emphatic assertion that 'the day of platform preachers is over'. Permit me a considered and measured response to this statement. Bunk!

I am convinced that there has never been a greater need for biblical literacy than today. If this can be facilitated by our gathering together to hear a thoughtful, well-prepared presentation that will ground us more on solid rock, then why not? Some churches are filled with prophetic junkies, eager for the next 'word', yet almost

repelled by the offer of an exposition. Ask them to turn
to chapter and verse, and eyes glaze over with disinter-
est. Suggest that you have a picture in your mind and
dress your message in prophetic frills, and you'll catch
their interest quickly.

God give us a revival of preaching, but preaching in
the order of Jesus. Let it be colourful, energetic, relevant,
and down-to-earth-yet-touched-by-heaven preaching.
Away with the parson's voice and the monotone drone.
Let the children understand and be delighted by winsome preaching, and may the adults find comfort,
equipping and challenge in it too.

In short, we need help. Lord Jesus, please teach us
how to preach.

EVANGELISM

THE MAD LOGIC OF THE DAY

'Hello, my name is Jeff . . . '

The passenger in the next seat fastened her seat belt, smiled, and told me that she was Laura, and that she was a San Francisco based clinical psychotherapist. Hmmm. This woman had serious brains. We could have a fascinating time of discussion to while the long flight hours away. I decided not to tell her what I did. Not yet. So I asked if she was a specialist in any particular area. Her answer froze the blood in my veins.

'I like to help Christians to get out of Christianity.'

I looked past the soft grin, and for a mad moment of over-reaction thought that I saw a vampire in her eyes. She asked me what I did for a living, and I was immediately tempted to advise her that I was a plumber, specializing in helping blockages to get out of sinks.

I took a deep breath, told her what I do, and added, 'I like to help people who are not Christians get into Christianity.' There, I had said it. Her face twisted in a scowl, her words coming now in sharp, staccato bursts, verbal machine gun at the shoulder.

'How can you believe all that stuff; all that "I am the way, the truth, the life" drivel? Those ideas are absolute statements. I don't believe in *any* absolutes. Does *anybody* these days?'

The last question stung, with its unsubtle inference that *nobody* but an alien from the planet Throg, who had perhaps been lobotomised, would pursue a life based on absolute truth – as the Christian does. On the back foot momentarily, I recovered and sent a volley back over the net, asking her if she was *sure* (absolutely sure?) that she didn't believe in absolutes?

She affirmed that it was so (eh?), and that, by way of illustration, affirmed that we might actually not be sitting on an aircraft, seeing as the declaration, 'I am in an aircraft' is an absolute idea. I ventured, perhaps mischievously, that we might perhaps therefore being flying at 36,000 feet in a large boat, or maybe even an orange or some other piece of soft fruit, and she agreed that I might well be right. I wondered if she might need to make an appointment to see herself, but to say so would have been crass and disrespectful, so I didn't mention it.

The flight was a fascinating, but mildly disturbing ride. Our discussion was warm and respectful, but the dialogue put a cloud over my heart. I left the plane feeling like a dinosaur, an out-of-touch fossil whose faith belonged to yesteryear and should have been buried in the name of progress. She tried to convince me that believing in God was a ridiculous notion: one that was intellectually bankrupt, one so philosophically unreasonable and untenable. I wasn't shaken at all by her arguments, but her tone made me feel like I was the irrational one, that any kind of assurance or conviction was unworthy in the modern market-place of vagueness, pluralism and relativism. I felt overwhelmed, not by the strength of the debate, but by the knowledge that our culture is totally drenched in this kind of 'woolly is good' thinking, where conviction is often viewed with the same suspicion as fundamentalism – which is the new blasphemy since the tragedy of the attack on the Twin Towers.

We live in a time when pages and pages of newspaper print are given over to the insane drivel that is astrology.

One might feel surprised that so many would even give lip service to the notion that their lives are affected by the geographical relative proximities of the planets, but nonetheless, millions scan those columns daily. Of course, astrology has a secret ingredient of success: it allows the existence of a higher power, without making a single moral demand upon any of us. It gives us a sense of higher destiny without a shred of discipleship or cost: perhaps this is the reason for the obsession.

Living for Christ in the multi-faith market-place isn't easy. It takes grace, wisdom, patience – as well as courage and boldness. But let the wise be seen as fools, and the philosophers as mumbling, incoherent, blind guides. I want to be with Jesus, with all of his certainty and sacrifice. Let them tell us that we're lost in space and mad for believing. I want to stay with the beacon of light that he truly is, in this fogbound culture that is ours.

THE GROUP

My palms were sweaty, and my voice trembled with nervousness as I looked around the small circle of men and women. It was my turn to speak.

'Hello everybody . . . my name is Jeff.' I paused, momentarily paralysed, feeling unable to make the terrible admission. The group leader nodded encouragement, willing me to go on.

Stammering slightly, I breathed in deeply, and repeated my introduction: 'My name is Jeff . . . and I'm an evangelist.'

'Hi Jeff,' they replied in sympathetic unison, smiles of relief all round.

They'd all been where I was now; they knew the pain of the first step. Encouraged by their warmth, I plunged into my tragic story. Holding nothing back, I described my downhill journey.

It had all begun so innocently – I had just wanted to see people make a response to Jesus. I told everyone I could about him; often disappearing behind the bike sheds at school to craftily share the good news with anyone who would listen. Then I got into tracts. I would wander the littered streets of our town every Saturday night, urgently pushing them to anyone who would take them. I was hooked. I purchased the largest evangelistic badge I could find, which screamed the message from my lapel. Huge black letters on a fluorescent orange background yelled the in-your-face question – 'Eternity: smoking or non-smoking?'

But soon I found that personal witnessing was not enough: it just didn't satisfy me any longer. I got into the big stuff. Intoxicated with mission fervour, I began travelling and preaching, longing, frantic even, to see people come to Christ. And then the classic character features of my calling began to kick in. I started to hang around with others like me, eating curries late into the night in different towns where I preached. My personal morality slipped. I became money hungry. I lost a grip on the truth. I found myself distanced from my local church, a travelling maverick. There was only one thing to do, if I was to emerge from my terrible addiction. I had to face the truth of what I had become. *I was an Evangelist*. And now, at the weekly meeting of the EA – *Evangelists Anonymous* – I poured out my sorry tale.

Of course, what you have just read is a complete myth, but I penned it to illustrate the very real truth that the word 'evangelist' has often been smeared, and the people with that calling have themselves been unhelpfully caricatured as a result. Despite my insistence that my calling is that of a Bible teacher (surely a more respectable tag), I'm often introduced as an evangelist – particularly when I go to the United States. In America, just about any Christian who owns a suitcase is an evangelist – and the fact that people often decide to become Christians when I speak, coupled with my own luggage collection, means that I have the 'E' tag. I wince when people introduce me thus, because to be an evangelist is no longer a respectable occupation in America – you might as well announce that your first name is Saddam. In the popular view, evangelists are those people who preach against pornography publicly and hang out with prostitutes privately. The more aggressive hucksters who beg for offerings from their viewers are collectively known as 'Television *Evangelists*', even though most of

them are Bible teachers – of a sort. It's not as bad in
Britain, but even here, evangelists sometimes labour
under negative caricatures. Evangelists typically exag-
gerate the numbers of people who either attend or
respond at their meetings, or so the rumour goes, so
we've developed the somewhat cheesy Christian pun
about evangelists speaking *evang-elastically*. Others seem
to think that the evangelist is a hit-and-run calling, a
mouth without a heart. In my experience, nothing could
be further from the truth.

Sure, I've met the odd maverick, whose character
doesn't match his or her gift. And I've met evangelists
who become a little over-enamoured with their impor-
tance in the kingdom. I'll never forget the guy who
handed me his business card: 'God Has Something to
Say to You Today if Only You'll Listen Ministries' was
the natty name of his organisation. And I've seen evangelists do and say some silly things – particularly when
it comes to the end of their sermon and they are 'throwing the net out' for a response. 'If you're here tonight'
they'll say, conveniently forgetting that everyone who is
there tonight is, well, there tonight.

Sometimes, desperate for response, evangelists can
make silly appeals. Initially inviting people to volunteer
for martyrdom via an excruciatingly agonizing death,
they have been known to descend to, 'Well come forward if you'd like to do a bit better in your Christian
life', or 'If you've ever eaten breakfast, please come forward' and even, 'Get down the front here if you've ever
cleaned your teeth – or even wanted to'. My friend Pete
Gilbert – a fine evangelist, as it happens – once witnessed an altar call where people who were making a
response to Jesus were invited to wink one eye!

But having hung around with a fair number of evangelists over the years, my discovery is that the vast

majority of them are passionate, committed people who often spend hundreds of lonely hours trekking around the country to sometimes tiny churches who pay them in book tokens. They *do* care – that's why they preach with such passion. And they *are* addicted to the noble cause. Like Paul, their cry is, 'I am compelled to preach . . . woe to me if I do not preach the gospel' (1 Cor. 9:16).

So please pray for those with the calling of evangelist: they have the joy of doing the work that makes angels party – leading sinners to repentance – but they also do that which makes the enemy wild with anger.

And refuse the caricature – we urgently and desperately need these priceless women and men who carry the call of evangelist, and not just because we need enthusiasts. Without them, the lost stay that way. Lost.

RELIGION

A REACTIONARY PEOPLE?

'I intend to give you all a jolly good ashing!' the Bishop chortled with a broad smile.

We looked around the boardroom nervously. The business meeting was drawing to a close, and we had agreed that we would conclude our time with some prayer, but now the Bishop's announcement took us by surprise. Mild panic came over us all, especially those who had misheard him and thought that he had announced a desire to give us all a good *thrashing*. Visions of *Tom Brown's Schooldays* swept into my mind, and I suppressed a temptation to shout 'I say, Flashman, there's been some ragging in the dorm!' at the top of my voice.

Undeterred by our nervous titters, the Bishop produced a cork, a box of matches, and a prayer book. Only when he had set fire to the cork, his smiling eyes reflected in the flames like a religious arsonist, did some of us realize that he was talking about *ashing*.

It was, of course, Ash Wednesday, and so Bishop Pete led us in a liturgy that celebrated the grace of God for a humanity that is, in a sense, nothing more than ash – and then wandered around the room, praying for us, that we in our raw nothingness would discover the outrage of grace, the reality of the King lifting up the beggar. Tears of gratitude and repentance flowed. It was rich.

Since then, I've been using the Anglican prayer book as a basis for my prayers, sometimes first thing in the morning, and sometimes in the closing moments before sleep. It feels a bit awkward, as I feel compelled to do the responses all by myself: 'The Lord be with you. *And also with you.*' It seems a little strange to begin each day by exchanging a greeting and a blessing with myself, the first sign of madness perhaps? But in encountering the power of liturgy, I made the simple discovery that I don't pray more than I do because I simply can't think of anything useful to say. To take the carefully thought through words of another, words that leap and dance with biblical truth, words that have been the comfort of believers through the centuries, has added another dimension to my spirituality. So what's going on? Am I becoming an undercover Anglican?

I think that, more to the point, I'm finding out that a lot of my pursuit of non-religious Christianity has been based on unhealthy reaction. It is brain-numbingly easy to define your Christianity in terms of what you *don't do*, so legalistic believers have a tendency to announce their pedigree as a result of having a list of things that they abstain from, thereby marking them as authentic. I've done that, along with many others, in the realm of non-religiosity. I've looked at what I saw as a religious style – pews/clerical dress/altars/candles/icons/liturgy and a host of other practices – and have thrown them all into a large skip called 'religion'. That skip is a fat, squat testament to my own arrogance – and also a huge amount of self-deception. In rejecting the traditions of others as being *religious*, I therefore set up my own habits and expressions of faith as being *alternative, radical, and non-religious*, and engage in one of the primary attitudes of the truly religious heart – pride – in the process. Ironically, having filled the skip, we have then had to scrabble around to find alternatives to what we have dumped.

So why, for example, do some of us have flags? Simple. In some of our traditions we don't have any stained glass windows. The colour and story-telling of religious architecture offers us some revelatory sunshine on an otherwise dreary day; when we look at a window or a symbol, the story comes alive for us. But we've put the windows in the skip, and installed our own boring UPVC new church-style worship that rejected any kind of colour and symbol with a neo-Puritan fervency. We jigged up and down in our draughty, tedious rented school halls, and got hugely bored. There was no smell of incense for us, just the faint odour of stale milk from the kitchens. And then, tired of our sterile, clinical religion, we made some flags: a bit of colour on canvas, and I'm glad we did. We were trying in a small way to break out of the scandal that is the divine made dull; to move away from the numbing condition that Annie Dillard laments:

'Week after week I was moved by the pitiableness of the bare linoleum floored sacristy which no flowers could cheer or soften, by the terrible singing I so loved, by the fatigued Bible readings, the lagging emptiness and dilution of the liturgy, the horrifying vacuity of the sermon, and by the fog of senselessness pervading the whole, which existed alongside, and probably caused, the wonder of the fact that we came; we returned; we showed up; week after week we went through with it . . . '[1]

We reacted, and congratulated ourselves that we were radical in the process. Perhaps there's a humility coming to us these days, a genuine sense that we really can enjoy the traditions of others.

---

[1] *Teaching a Stone to Talk* – Annie Dillard

But even there, there's another danger. It's possible that we might over-react and take just about anything on board in the desperate desire to see something – anything – happen. The somewhat exasperating ability of God to come running wherever he finds a hungry people is frustrating to those of us who just want to know 'whether it's right – or wrong'. It is confusing until we remind ourselves that he operates the same policy towards fallen *us*. But his blessing and activity in no way mandates or confirms his approval of everything that is done there. He calls us to ask gracious, mature questions, rather than to swallow, wholesale, everything that is done in his name.

So let's neither react and consign other people's practices to the garbage, or just put our brains on hold in a 'never mind the quality, feel the width' approach to revival. Reflection, rather than reaction, will produce light rather than heat.

I have to go now. I've got a big skip that I'm currently rifling through.

HOW TO BE A CHRISTIAN – *NOT*

They were, to coin a phrase, *'very spiritual'*. Always first in line when it came to praying, and renowned for their street ministries, they embodied a zealous godliness that certainly turned heads. Rumour had it that they prayed for three hours daily. Their faith was steel like and solid; they had no truck with woolly, liberal theology, but had a firm grip on the doctrines of resurrection and judgement, and of angels and demons. They could accurately quote Scripture with smooth ease.

They were fiery, roaring revivalists. Not for them the morgue-cold cynicism that expects little or nothing from heaven. They were always on tiptoe, expecting God to move at any time, and called sinners to repent and make ready for his coming. Members of a holiness movement, their hope fuelled them in their almost pernickety obsession with personal purity. Despising foggy compromise, they thundered that God was either Lord of all, or not Lord at all. Every little detail of life must come under his control.

Impressed?

They were the Pharisees.

Today, those of us who are preachers tend to set the Pharisees up as easy targets, as punch bags handy for a quick Sunday morning jab. Like the wicked witches in the pantomime that we love to hiss and boo at, the Pharisees have generally been painted in an entirely negative light, like wholly religious crones.

But their faults were not always so obvious, and they were uncomfortably like us, like modern evangelical Christians. A lay movement formed around 200 years before Christ, the Pharisees, had embraced an approach to spirituality that was hallmarked by passion and dedication. They would even gather together for conventions for mutual encouragement. I imagine that a *Spring Harvest: Pharisees Together at Butlins* event would have been a little short on fun . . .

Their closest allies were the Scribes, or 'the teachers of the law' as Matthew tags them. They were that strange mixture of commitment mingled with dullness that can still be evidenced by spiritual people today. Generally thought of as dry, uninspiring preachers who knew a lot, but lacked spiritual authority, they were also great students of Scripture. Their pursuit of 'law trivia' enabled the Scribes to announce that there were 613 commandments in the first 5 books of the Old Testament: 248 positive, and 365 negative. This microscopic approach to Scripture demanded infinite precision and commitment to detail – which meant that they often lost sight of the plot, fighting over detail and missing the big picture by miles.

Surely there would have been Pharisees and Scribes standing in the crowd on that epic day when Jesus delivered his Sermon on the Mount. Mental notebooks open, sharpened pencils poised, they would have listened carefully to his every word, they would have listened as a self appointed jury for the prosecution. Brows furrowed in stern concentration, they would have evaluated and analysed each statement, testing its 'soundness', and ready to pounce at the slightest hint of what they perceived as error. Any ordinary, common people in the crowd that day would have given them a wide berth. The Scribes and the Pharisees had an intimidating, white-hot religion that seemed to scald those lower down the religious food chain. The Scribes and the Pharisees herded people smeared with failure and shame into the corral of but one indicting designation: 'sinners'. Theirs was a religiosity long on law, and short on compassion. But surely they were to be commended for their zeal?

Apparently not. When Jesus gave his great sermon, it was not the 'sinners' who came under fire from his words. On the contrary, Jesus seemed to roll out a Kingdom red carpet for those who felt keenly their lack of God, the 'poor in spirit'. Stunningly, it was the full, not the hungry, those who appeared to own the established franchise on religion, the Scribes and Pharisees, who Jesus had in his sights for a judgement salvo. Far from holding them up as exemplary models of commitment and devotion, he slammed them with a repeated, exocet phrase: 'Don't be like them'. Their highest acts of devotion, in prayer, fasting and almsgiving were rejected by Jesus as useless. Elsewhere, he carefully warned his friends and would be apprentices about allowing, 'the leaven of the Pharisees' to creep into their own spirituality (Matthew 16:6). And no one can read the almost nuclear vocabulary of Matthew 23, where the Pharisees are tagged as 'vipers' and 'whitened tombs full of dead men's bones', without trembling.

When Jesus formed his team, not one of these experts in prayer or scripture were invited to join. Apparently, he preferred the unspoiled pliability of rough, ordinary working men and even the red-faced gratitude of former extortionists to the practised piety of the religious. The Pharisees were blinded by their own religion, rejecting the remarkable, supernatural ministry of Jesus, writing it off as sourced by dark power. Even the appearance of a still stinking Lazarus, raised to life now, didn't shake

them. Their principles had become more valued than
God's purposes: Jesus indicted them with the charge that
their traditions had become more important than the
commandments of God.

And so it becomes clear that there is a *religiosity* that can
hijack those who would be holy. I have observed that this
'leaven' of religiosity is the primary temptation for those
who would be among Jesus' most committed followers.
Like a devastating computer virus that mugs your hard
drive and then tries to automatically infect everyone on
your email address list, so religion crouches in the wings
whenever commitment or zealousness is in the air. It cor-
rupts, and seeks converts. Just as Islamic faith Bin Laden-
style is denounced as being a corruption of true Islam, so
there is a mutated, religious Christianity that is loud, critical of others, passionate and almost martyr-like – but is a
fundamentalism that we should avoid at all costs.
'Religious' Christianity is worse than useless. It deters
those who are genuinely looking for God, repelled, as they
will surely be, by a church preoccupied with stern priva-
tized piety and empty irrelevance. This is a faith useless to
the world – and impotent before God. Religion's fervent
praying goes unheard in heaven, according to Jesus.

But it takes great grace to be a Christian without being
religious. Face it, we all have some of it in us. If you want
to know if you have some of that 'leaven', there's a simple test: just take your pulse. If you're alive, it's more
than likely that you have at least some of the virus
pumping through your spiritual veins. Ask God to give
you a health check today, and put in a request for real,
living, humble faith, and not the sham imitation that is
so readily available. God has no affection for mere religion. On the contrary, I think that he hates it.

The Pharisees were experts at what Gerard Kelly calls
'pray and display'. They dressed to make a religious

fashion statement, adorned with 'tephillin': small leather boxes containing portions of scripture, which screamed, '*Don't you know I love Scripture*'. And tassels: the four tassels from the prayer shawl which, likewise, made a statement, '*Back off everyone, here comes an intercessor.*'

Impressive it was, and hollow too. Jesus dismissed this posturing as the work of 'hypocrites'. Matthew uses that word no less than thirteen times. Palestine had some fine theatres – one was located in the city of Sepphoris, within a few miles of Jesus' home of Nazareth. Perhaps Jesus, as a boy, saw the 'hypocrites', the actors who worked there, prancing about the stage in their masks and sometimes giving running commentaries on the play. Other *hypocrites* were employed to professionally, 'turn on the waterworks', as it were, at funerals. They would weep and wail for the unknown departed, and tear their clothes along the seams, so they could quickly stitch them up again for the next funeral performance. The word 'hypocrite' gradually crept into common usage to describe anyone who was a pretender.

Gordon MacDonald has described pretending as the 'common cold of the evangelical church'. Religion that relies on us having weekly close encounters of an evangelical kind, working hard at the sweaty business of unreality, reeks of religion. Do you want real, true religion? Then get real, at least with somebody.

Jesus drew an almost Pythonesque sketch when he describes the Pharisees as giving, while blowing trumpets to announce the fact. This kind of spiritual posturing was roundly condemned in the great sermon. Jesus was not rejecting the validity of public and communal expressions of spirituality. Some have rejected the idea of corporate prayer gatherings, or a call to collective fasting, because of a misunderstanding of this teaching. But public platforms and prayer meetings are particularly toxic

zones for the bacteria of religion: all of us should negoti-
ate them with care.

Mere religion is a corruption of true faith, and is part
of a satanic biochemical campaign. Be humble about
your own tradition, and respectful of others. Avoid
masks and performances, and take notice when you're
being noticed. Be alert and careful. For God's sake.

The Ministry of Silly Walks was one of the all-time
Monty Python classics. The sketch gave us the unforgettable vision of a gangly John Cleese, splendid with
bowler hat and brolly, prancing and high-kicking his
way along the High Street. The genius was in the bizarre
absurdity of it all. In other famous Python sketches,
there's a football match that featured the London
Gynaecologists; a very dead parrot was returned to a pet
shop, whose owner insisted that the rigid bird was just
sleeping; and the Spanish Inquisition that no one expect-
ed, was led by the hapless Cardinal Fang. The images are
memorable because they are ridiculous in the extreme.

Consider the Sermon on the Mount: was the genius of
Python a borrowed gift? There we are treated to images
of religious philanthropists who have a team of trum-
peters on call, eager to sound the reveille whenever a
coin is dropped in the offering. There are other more
ascetic types who make themselves down rather than
up, colouring themselves ugly just to let everyone know
that it's fasting time again. And droning street-corner
prayer warriors blether on at length, while all the time
God isn't listening anyway . . .

These too are visual exaggerations (borrowed from
the strange but true, real life practices of the Pharisees),
caricatures sketched to grab our attention and expose a
form of religiosity that we must avoid like the plague.

So ask for a holy inoculation, and beware the virus of the
Pharisees: they show us how to live the life of faith. *Not*.

TURN THAT VOLUME DOWN

Three hundred years ago, I attended a Bible College: at least it feels that long ago now. I shared a dormitory with a wide-eyed, zealous chap whose passion for all things spiritual was renowned. In our weekly college prayer meetings, he would always do a turn, roaring his prayers in the manner of Ian Paisley, with plenty of King James Version quotations stitched in, in an impressive tapestry. He only had one volume setting: loud. Whether he was debating some theological detail in a lecture, or preaching in the sermon class, he would bark, rant, and chop out his words staccato style, and he seemed to particularly relish any opportunity to yell about hell. One got the distinct impression that this chap's God was just trembling with joyous anticipation at the thought of treating most of humanity to an eternal barbecue. He also had moments of softness and vulnerability, and could, on occasion, be a thoroughly nice chap, but all too often, he would revert to a rather ugly hardness. One time, he got into a fierce theological argument about the nature of salvation with another student. Would the saved be preserved forever without possibility of losing their salvation? And were the followers of Jesus the elect, the ones personally hand-picked by God before the beginning of time. The row rumbled on, and suddenly flared up like a forest fire, and we were treated to the sight of these two hotheads in a fight, punching home their convictions by punching each other.

I hadn't seen my high-octane colleague for years, until a couple of months ago, when he made a totally unexpected appearance on Sky News. At the risk of sounding like Victor Meldrew, I could hardly believe it. David Trimble was trying to make a speech, and a gaggle of unruly members of the Northern Irish Assembly were pushing and shoving each other in a now famous punch-up. And there, right in the middle of it all, eyes ablaze and fingers jabbing, was my erstwhile friend – his ire undiluted by the years. It was a sorry sight.

'Religious' people can be quite accomplished in the enthusiasm department, and their passion and vehement certainty can intimidate us, silencing our disquiet about their views as they smother us with zeal. But with things spiritual, loud is not necessarily good. The Pharisees were undeniably committed to their cause, praying with ear splitting passion and pursuing Jesus with pernickety questions with the doggedness of Sherlock Holmes. But their zeal was a twisted, warped and even ugly thing. As we realize that Paul shook his head with shame as he remembered his religiously zealous past, so we must know that those who shout aren't necessarily right. God is looking for true sincerity of heart, and is not impressed by the decibel level of the misguided fanatic. So, Jesus instructs us to pray with thoughtfulness, rather than 'babbling on with vain repetitions'. This is no prohibition against liturgy; repetition is not the enemy here. Rather, it's *vain* repetition that is met with a yawn from heaven. When you are told by a livid, 'righteously indignant' enthusiast that you need to do discipleship *his* way, then don't back away from the blast. Verbosity doesn't necessarily equal orthodoxy.

And be careful when you sense a calling to put everyone else right, to be the 'watchman', God's ever ready instrument of correction. Some people know how to bruise others without ever actually throwing a punch. As they do so, they highlight the small sins of others, and become character murderers in the process.

Unhelpfully 'religious' people usually carry a microscope around with them. The Pharisees were meticulous. Exalting nit-picking to an art form, they were proud of their habit of giving a tenth of the produce of their spice gardens – a practice never required by the law – but they blatantly ignored more important matters, like justice, mercy and faithfulness. Religion is rife when churches and individuals select specific rules and regulations – most of which have nothing to do with actual biblical requirements – as a way of measuring who is 'in' and who is 'out'. The Pharisees apparently developed detailed regulations about how much one should greet a bride on her wedding day, how to commiserate with a widow at a funeral, and even a restriction about looking into a mirror on the Sabbath. Real danger lingered with mirror use: one might discover a grey hair – and then, horror of horrors, there would be the temptation to remove the hair – and that would constitute working on the Sabbath.

Sound mindless? I visited a church once where a visiting speaker had announced his 'revelation' that genuinely holy women would stop shaving their legs, by order. Once again, legalism had struck a blow against women. In fiercely religious churches, it's normally the women who are first in line for oppression and control, because legalism is a sexist spirit. Of course, the church must be a community that commits itself to living out the ethics of Jesus. Without that commitment, we will never fulfil our calling to be a lighthouse people. But whenever matters of personal choice or conscience – where there is no clear biblical imperative – become legislated and controlled, there is mere religion rearing its ugly head. Legalism is lazy. A church community that dictates the minutiae of personal behaviour actually develops people who lose the ability to think for themselves. A vibrant personal friendship with God is not necessary in this kind of church: we can just lean on the rule book that others have drafted. Don't stand for it, and don't silence your awkward questions because you risk being tagged as rebellious or divisive. Ask away, and think these issues through for yourself, because mindless legalism shouldn't be tolerated. It handcuffs believers, puts an obscene mask on the face of a loving God, and makes Christianity repulsive and irrelevant to those who are genuinely seeking the truth.

The Pharisees were also very good at being loudly offended: incensed with Jesus because he didn't wash his hands in the highly dramatic manner required by tradition. Ironically, they saw no problem with their own plotting of his death. 'Religious' people strain at the gnats of others faults, while gulping down the camels of their own shortcomings. In another Pythonesque word sketch, we see them diligently searching for the tiniest speck in the eye of another, while oblivious to planks the size of coffee tables that are sticking out of their own heads. Once again, the irony is that sometimes those who shout the loudest are those whose lives least represent the values of the Kingdom. Legalistic Christianity is loaded with loud hailing holiness preachers who, to borrow the words of Jesus, 'do not practice what they preach. They tie up heavy loads and put them on men's shoulders, but they themselves are not willing to lift a finger to move them' (Matt. 23:3–4).

Religious Christianity almost seems to relish any opportunity to criticise and disqualify others. Like an umpire who yells, 'You're out!' at a failed batsman, so the religious seem to inflate their own sense of being right by the insistence that almost everybody else is wrong. Some of the most 'pious' people that I've encountered are also gifted prosecuting attorneys. Life for them has become a lifelong crusade of correcting others. They are the self-appointed watchmen and women who demand that everyone else must look and live like them.

That's not to say that we should never make judgements. The quote, 'Do not judge, lest you be judged', is one of the most misunderstood verses in the Bible. Right judgement, at a corporate and state level, is vital: our society would unravel without it. Church discipline is impossible unless we are willing to say that certain behaviour is inconsistent with being a member of the Christian community – and that requires judgement.

But it was the propensity of the Pharisees to pass *corrupt* judgements that earned them such a stinging series of rebukes from Jesus. They grabbed the woman caught in adultery by the scruff of the neck, and hurled her into the arena of debate, like a defiled court exhibit – but where was the man who obviously participated in that shamed couple's joint sin? And the Pharisees tended to smear entire people groups with prejudiced name-calling: 'Why do you eat with tax collectors and sinners?' We can be tempted to tiptoe around compulsively offended people, who often use the injunction that we should 'not stumble the weaker brother' as a catch-all to make sure that their personal sensibilities are never violated. But perhaps we would better serve the 'offence addict' if we shared the idea that some maturity and grace on their part would be in order.

The cross of Christ is an instrument of liberation, not a mechanism to enslave us to a crushed, joyless life. For those who would follow Jesus with the greatest enthusiasm, mere 'religion' lingers as our primary temptation.

Like sin, it crouches at the door, and desires to master us. Be alert, and be diligent.

'Be careful', Jesus said to his disciples. 'Be on your guard against the yeast of the Pharisees and Sadducees' (Matthew 16:6).

JOSIE BECKHAM

It was a *beautiful* shot, the kind of heavenly volley that sends football commentators into verbal overdrive; a punt to launch a brace of slow-motion action replays. The ball rolled gently towards the player, who eyed it nervously at first. Tension crackled in the crowd. Suddenly, as if anointed by genius, the player stepped back on their right heel, and performed a *coup de grâce* kick. Hands outstretched aeroplane-like, poise and balance perfect, foot connected perfectly with leather with a deep, solid thud, scooping it up in a bend-it-like-Beckham power drive. It was surely sheer soccer poetry. Somewhere in the distance, a huge crowd rose to their feet as one, and gave a deafening cheer. The player, lost in the moment, was oblivious to their roar of approval.

The minister looked on, staggered. This was *most* unexpected, for this perfect kick was not performed in a stadium or park, but in the main meeting hall – *the sanctuary*, some would call it – of a church in mid Wales. It was late Sunday evening when it happened. Most of the congregation was enjoying that chatty cuppa-in-hand *bonhomie*, the warm afterglow ritual that caps ten thousand Sunday evening services. The minister watched, feeling the pleasurable tired ache that comes when the sun sets on yet another busy Sunday, enjoying the clinking sound of china and the relaxed atmosphere. The service that had just concluded had been a happy affair. There had been a refreshing cocktail of laughter and tears, and a challenge given that we should *think* about our faith, and not just keep doing the same old things simply because, well, that's what we do. Grace was in the air.

One of the children had been playing with a ball when it happened. The football rolled across the fading carpet to Josie, a sprightly lady of 70, faithful to God and this church for the past 55 years. What would she do? Perhaps a gentle rebuke about the evils of playing soccer in church buildings?

Josie was the player. She eyed the ball hungrily, and for a few seconds she was 16 years old again, and a member of the local girls soccer team. She had loved the game dearly; perhaps she was a local star. And then, as she put it, 'She got saved'. Fraternising with 'the world' was not encouraged, and sports were considered 'worldly'. To have continued on the team would have meant violating the prohibitionist doctrine of separation that was preached at the time. And so, Josie hung up her soccer boots for the last time, and had not kicked a ball for over half a century. There was no angst, for she was not bitter about her loss. She turned her back on the game, and threw all of her energies into the life of the church.

And then that late Sunday night ball appeared before her. As Josie said later, 'something from the past rose up within me.' So, she performed a masterful kick. The minister's mouth fell open, first with amazement, and then admiration.

'I realize now that a lot of the things that we were told were sin, weren't really', she explained later with a warm smile.

And as I heard her story, I wondered about the countless Christians that I still meet, for whom faith has been less than liberating. Too often, I bump into good, kind, sincere believers who are passionately committed to a message of freedom, but who have been squeezed into the painful corsets of fear by second hand, unthinking dogma. They are the ones who believe in joy, but are nervous of laughter. It is they who occasionally doubt (as all humans do) but feel like they would be committing a Judas-like act of betrayal if they admitted their struggles. They are those for whom everything in life has to be productive, efficient, and spiritually significant. They have left spontaneity and play – and simple down-to-earth *fun* – like discarded toys of their childhood, rejected now for a stern, almost obsessive discipleship. They need to kick a ball; build a sandcastle; laugh out loud; face their uncertainties; giggle on a Sunday.

As I conclude this second *Lucas on Life*, I wonder if perhaps heaven is waiting for the locked up ones to get a bit more – of a life. And when they take those small steps of freedom, heaven notices, and somewhere in the distance, a huge crowd rises to their feet as one, and gives a deafening cheer. And the player, lost in the moment, is oblivious to their roar of approval.

If you would like details of audio and video teaching tapes by Jeff Lucas, or would like further information about any aspect of his ministry, please contact

www.jefflucas.org

ALSO AVAILABLE BY

JEFF LUCAS FROM

AUTHENTIC LIFESTYLE

LUCAS ON LIFE

'Life, even the Christian life, is not a gallop from one
thrill to another – there are the boring bits. Jesus has
washed my sins away, but I still have to wash the car.
Grinning with gritted teeth doesn't work when tragedy
knocks on your door. Jesus didn't flash a cheesy smile
and head-butt a tambourine in Gethsemane. He struggled, wept, ached and argued – and stayed faithful to his
father's will. He was open about his pain, begging his
sleepy friends to watch in prayer with him. Reality
– not unending ecstasy – is required.'

In *Lucas on Life*, Jeff takes you on a memorable journey
through life's ups and downs, pointing out lessons that
need to be learned on the way.

ISBN: 1-86024-360-6

HOW NOT TO PRAY

Jeff Lucas sets out, in his own inimitable style, to debunk those myths that turn prayer into purgatory and stop us from enjoying the relationship with God that we were meant for. The myths include: believing that prayer is only about us – and believing that prayer is never about us; that the only good prayers are long prayers that we can't pray anyway, and that God is both far off and reluctant to hear us. Written with humour and passion, this is an immensely readable and helpful book that will delight those who have discovered the joys of Jeff Lucas' writings before, as well as those who come to it fresh.

ISBN: 1-85078-452-3